GOD
Is a Man of
WAR

The Problem of Violence
in the Old Testament

REV. DR. STEPHEN DE YOUNG

ANCIENT FAITH PUBLISHING

CHESTERTON, INDIANA

God is a Man of War: The Problem of Violence in the Old Testament
Copyright © 2021 Stephen De Young

PUBLISHED BY:

Ancient Faith Publishing
A Division of Ancient Faith Ministries
P.O. Box 748
Chesterton, IN 46304

ISBN: 978-1-955890-04-5

Library of Congress Control Number: 2021945444

Printed in the United States of America

Table of Contents

CONTENTS

Preface

FEW ASPECTS OF THE SCRIPTURES challenge modern sensibilities more than the violence found particularly in the Old Testament narratives. Atheists draw out the most brutal events in the Old Testament—from the narratives or the commandments of the Torah—and present them in the most shocking way possible as a way to attack the message of the Scriptures wholesale. Modern Christians and skeptics alike are offended by these texts that violate their consciences, rarely realizing that, ironically, their sense of right and wrong has itself been shaped by the Christian message.

It warrants mentioning at the outset that this book contains depictions of violence that, while originating in both scriptural and historical texts, may be disturbing to some. Admittedly, a book on violence in the Bible is not easy to write for various reasons, not the least of which is that we live in a broken world. Many who come to this topic have had their own encounters with violence that have left them wounded or even disturbed. The intention behind this book is neither to sensationalize nor minimize those passages in the Bible that testify to the reality of violence, nor to expunge them from the living witness of Holy Scripture simply because they make us uncomfortable on a gut level. Instead, *God Is a Man of War* seeks to better understand and thereby integrate these passages within our understanding of the Scriptures and God's active presence within and throughout the course of human experiences, including our own.

In the ancient Church, the heretic Marcion proposed that Yahweh, the God of Israel in the Hebrew Scriptures, was a fundamentally different—and more malevolent—God than the Father of Jesus Christ. This extreme conclusion, that the God described by the Old Testament was evil by the standards of the New, was followed by later forms of Gnosticism. While few commentators alive today would call themselves "Marcionite," the rhetoric of both atheists who seek to invalidate the Bible in its entirety and self-identified Christians who invalidate certain elements or portions of the Scriptures echo Marcion's language regarding the God of the Old Testament. Even well-meaning commentators sometimes regard the Old Testament, and specifically the violence it contains, as something of an embarrassment, an arcane relic from the distant past. As such, they argue that it should be "unhitched" or ignored altogether in the Christian proclamation.[1]

Unlike Marcion, this book operates from the premise that Yahweh, the God of Israel, is the Holy Trinity. The various figures of the Old Testament, as recorded there, had real contact with and experience of the Son and Word of God, His Father, and His Spirit. The descriptions of these encounters as recorded in the Scriptures are accurate and not the product of human speculation, theologizing, or

---

1   This book is not aimed directly at arguing against Marcionism by identifying the Holy Trinity as Yahweh, the God of both Old and New Testaments. For Marcion himself to make the case that these are two different gods, he could recognize the authority of only one Gospel and a handful of Pauline epistles. Even these, in Marcion's case, were particular versions of those texts that do not match those currently exercising canonical authority in the Church. There is no meaningful reading of the Christian New Testament that can support the conclusion that there are two different gods issuing the two covenants. For further discussion of the Holy Trinity in the Old Testament, see my previous book, *The Religion of the Apostles.*

other reasoning. At the same time, the same accounts occasionally expressed, originated from, or resulted in violence. Instead of avoiding or invalidating these episodes out of discomfort, what happens when we inquire what these episodes—part and parcel of the totality of Scripture—might reveal about the nature of Christ and His creation? This is the guiding question behind *God Is a Man of War*.

All translations of the Scriptures and other ancient sources are my own. That said, no translation is ever perfect, and that includes the ones I present. Translation is more an art than a science, especially when working with ancient languages that are constructed very differently than the English language. Sometimes, in making a particular point or argument, a translation may need to be very precise about a certain word or explain that the same word is used in two places. For a variety of reasons, however, a standard English translation may lack that precision. For all these reasons it seems best to translate afresh for significant quotations.

Yahweh,
a Man of War

I N THE GREAT HYMN OF victory sung by the people of Israel after passing through the sea, they identify their God, the God who had delivered them, and His character. "Yahweh is *a man of war*, Yahweh is His name" (Ex. 15:3, emphasis added). The drowned Egyptian enemies had suffered a military defeat, though it was water that did the killing. This is neither the first time in the Scriptures that violent action is attributed to the God of Israel nor the last. Yet the notion of Yahweh as a "man of war" would become central to Israel's understanding of God as One who brings about justice. Indeed, the title *Yahweh Sabaoth*[1] is sometimes rendered as "Lord of hosts" and evokes Yahweh as the commander of armies and mighty in battle.

This is not merely an analogy or metaphor—God wrought actual, not illusory, violence upon the earth on numerous occasions. The Egyptian soldiers and the firstborn of their people and livestock lay dead. Prior to this, the cities of Sodom and Gomorrah had been consumed, along with their inhabitants. The judges of Israel, under the

---

1   Though it is sometimes confused with the word "Sabbath" in English, *Sabaoth* derives from a verb that means "to teem or be many." It refers to a large group or gathering of people, like an army; hence the phrasing "Lord of hosts."

influence of the Holy Spirit, would later kill Philistines by the hundreds at God's behest.

Importantly, Israel was not immune to the experience of God's violence. In the time of King Hezekiah of Judah, Yahweh sent first the Assyrians to slaughter the ten tribes of the Northern Kingdom of Israel, deport the survivors, and obliterate them ethnically. Then the Babylonians attacked the remnant of Judah and deported the survivors. Later, the Romans eradicated Judea and, for centuries, Jerusalem, from the face of the earth. The Romans first invaded Judea in AD 70, destroying the temple in Jerusalem and killing thousands. At the climax of the Bar Kochva rebellion in AD 136, the entire city of Jerusalem was destroyed, with a new Roman city built on top of the ruins. The Romans then enacted a ruthless de-Judaification policy across the entire region. These brutal events became the stuff of legend through the descriptions of contemporaries and were both prophesied and interpreted after the fact as being the judgment of Israel's God. In the Apocalypse of St. John, the future hope of Christians is one where Christ reaps the fields of the earth in wrath, churning up a torrent of blood as deep as a horse's bridle is high (Rev. 14:14–20).

Too often, those seeking to "salvage" the Scriptures—motivated by our modern disapproval of violence, particularly when it affects children and other innocents—are in actuality explaining away the Scriptures rather than seeking to understand them. When the Scriptures or elements of the Church's Tradition prove difficult, this is an invitation to delve into them more deeply, not to evade them. In this world, suffering, pain, and death—even of those who are blameless—are realities. This was not less true in the ancient world, but likely more so.

The value attributed to every human life from conception to grave is a Christian moral principle that emerges in Christ. The ancient world discriminated between different "qualities" of humans based on all manner of criteria and conducted themselves accordingly, victimizing and killing as the powerful deemed necessary. This was the reality in which ancient people, including the authors of Scripture, lived. Their encounters with God, then, were encounters between God and a world of this character, warts (and swords) and all, just as God encounters us today in our own imperfect world. Any understanding of violence in the Scriptures must therefore integrate rather than disassociate from the violence that exists in the world. It must account for the actual suffering, pain, and loss of real human persons who lived and died in this world and who knew and were known by Christ.

The Problem of Violence

THE ULTIMATE REVELATION OF THE Triune God is the Incarnation of Jesus Christ, God the Son. Christ is the lens through which all of the Scriptures, the ongoing life of the Church, and life in creation are understood. In Him is the fullness of deity in bodily form (Col. 2:9). It is perfectly correct to interpret the actions of Yahweh, the God of Israel in the Old Testament, in light of who we know Him to be through those who knew Christ and wrote the New Testament Scriptures. He is, after all, the same yesterday, today, and forever (Heb. 13:8).

Care must be taken, however, to ensure that the revelation of Christ is understood as a complete whole before such interpretation can commence. Examples of the powerful depths of Christ's love, compassion, humility, and kindness abound in the Gospels and other New Testament writings that reflect on Christ's life and ministry. Christ's sacrificial death stands clearly as the ultimate image of the love of God in the Scriptures and indeed in history. For many, these images are so overpowering that they become the entire picture.

This same Jesus Christ, however, rose from the grave triumphant over the powers of sin, death, and the devil. This same Christ cast demons into the abyss. This same Christ will tell those who did not share his compassion and love on the last day, "Be gone; I never knew you" (Matt. 7:23). This same Christ said of Judas that it would have been better for him to have never been born. This same Christ excoriated the hypocrisy of the Pharisees, drove the moneylenders out of the temple, and issued fierce diatribes against Herod, the chief priests, and the scribes. The Apocalypse of St. John depicts this same Christ leading the slaughter of His enemies. Indeed, the very title *Christ*, meaning "anointed one," identifies Him as the King who reigns over all creation, who judges the nations with an iron rod.

Further, the faithful of the Second Temple period (c. 515 BC to AD 70) and the earliest Christians believed that Christ, before His Incarnation, appeared and acted in the Old Testament. He, the second hypostasis, or Person, of Yahweh, the God of Israel, the second Person of the Holy Trinity, ate with Abraham at Mamre and then called down fire from the Father on Sodom and Gomorrah. He wrote the commandments of the Torah with His own finger on tablets, including all of their penalties. As the Angel of the Lord, He led the Israelites out of Egypt, through the wilderness, and in battle against the Egyptians and Amorites. As the Commander of Yahweh's armies, he led Joshua into battle against the giants in the land of Canaan. As the Word of Yahweh, He appeared to the prophets and pronounced judgment and doom upon entire civilizations.

For the New Testament authors, it is this already existing understanding of Christ in His majesty, in His power, in His glory that makes the humility, sacrifice, and compassion of Jesus so ineffably worthy of worship and awe. The great Christological hymn recorded by St. Paul, known as the *Carmen Christi*, marvels at this tension between the God of Israel in His glory and power, Yahweh Sabaoth, becoming man and going to His death on a Roman instrument of torture, a cross (Phil. 2:6–11). The deep truth of the Incarnation is not that a god took on human form. Rather, it is that Yahweh, the God of

4

Israel, the Creator of all things, the Lord of the powers, was born in a cave and laid in a feed trough, lived as a peasant outcast, and died condemned as a criminal.

The Jesus Christ of today's popular imagination, on the other hand, is a vastly diminished version of the One the saints knew. He has been wholly removed from the Old Testament, and the Apocalypse is largely ignored or dismissed as a sort of sectarian fever dream. To modern readers, even St. Paul appears in his epistles to be motivated by some different agenda than that of the Gospels. Interpreters of St. Paul's texts cite the lack of direct references to the events of Jesus' life or quotations from His teaching as evidence that Paul was engaged in speculative theology that has little to do with the "historical Jesus." The Resurrection, the culmination of the Gospel accounts, is no longer perceived as victory or conquest but as evidence that Christ's spirit, memory, or example would live on through the ages to inspire goodness and compassion in others. The infant Jesus in the manger is not a contradiction too deep to fathom by the human mind but the image of a child meek, sweet, and mild who can be adored safely from a distance and who would not harm a fly. This imaginary Jesus is not the God who created the universe, made flesh to save humanity by His power and might. Rather, he is a friendly and good-willed human who became a martyr.

Efforts to downplay the violence in the Hebrew Scriptures pit this more popular, sentimental Jesus against depictions of Yahweh in the Old Testament, who appears to be a rather different sort of God than Hallmark Christ.[2] The constructed contrast is sharpened by

---

2   Likely assisted by Martin Luther's distinction between Law and Gospel in the Scriptures, this depiction of Christ over against the warrior God of the Old Testament was already prevalent in nineteenth-century Germany among liberal scholars. Friedrich Nietzsche, in particular, decried not the comparison but the warm embrace of this form of Christ by his scholarly contemporaries. He, of course, much preferred the more regal and powerful God of the Old Testament.

the tendency to overlook the many passages, beginning with much of Deuteronomy in the Torah, that speak of Yahweh's love for His people and for humankind in general. The God of the Old Testament is depicted as all wrath, violence, and judgment, while Christ is depicted as an infant, a lamb, and a soft man dressed in soft clothing.[3]

The dissonance between contemporary understandings of the God of the Old and New Testaments constitutes the central problem this book seeks to address. Rather than squaring a violent Old Testament Yahweh with a tender Jesus Christ, the objective is to recover the fundamental Christian teaching that the God whom Jesus Christ represents and Yahweh—the God of the Old Testament—are one and the same. This doctrine was understood by the apostolic and subsequent generations of Christianity and has not changed. Jesus Christ is the ultimate revelation of God not in the sense of contradicting, correcting, or even adding to the previous revelation, but by being God, in Person, whom all previous revelation was describing. Experiences of God in the Old Testament that were of a violent character or that otherwise shock our contemporary sensibilities are not an exception.

Bad Answers

IT IS NECESSARY TO EXPLORE this cognitive gap between Old and New Testament understandings of God in order to better adjust our own thinking and understand the Scriptures more deeply. It is insufficient to simply assume that some characteristics—such

---

3   The widespread embrace by Protestantism of penal substitutionary atonement, sometimes even claiming that this view of atonement *is* the gospel, has only exacerbated this problem. The Father is depicted as being required by justice or by His own nature to punish all sin through the infliction of suffering and death. Christ is then cast as the eternal victim of this divine violence on our behalf.

as violence—correspond to Yahweh in the Old Testament, while others—like the Triune character of Father, Son, and Holy Spirit—correspond to the New. This assumption compromises the identity of the God of the Scriptures, potentially calling into question the entire biblical testimony.

So what do we do with the violence of the Old Testament? Popular theology is replete with poor answers to this question, some even with the backing of scholarship. They reflect a desire to "unhitch" the Old Testament and simply preach Christ risen from the dead as the more evangelistically appealing figure. Among the hallmarks of this approach is the assumption that the portrayal of God according to the Hebrew Scriptures is invalid. While scholars reach this conclusion from a variety of angles, they most commonly argue that the Hebrew Scriptures are a purely human product that reflects the thoughts of Bronze and Iron Age peoples about God but does not represent the authentic experience of Yahweh, the God of Israel. Within this view is a range of opinions concerning which portions of the Scriptures constitute authentic religious experience. Some affirm all but a few troublesome passages from the Old Testament as Scripture, while others concede only an occasional glimmer of the authentic revelation of Christ in the entire Hebrew Bible. The biggest problem with this approach is that it is contrived to fix a (supposed) problem—namely, the seemingly incongruous accounts of God between the two Testaments—rather than offer an explanation that proceeds from a consistent methodology. The sole criterion for repudiating a particular portion of text is that it offends contemporary sentiment. As such sentiments change over time, what is and isn't considered Scripture will fluctuate as well.

A further weakness of this approach is inconsistency: many adherents fail to apply this rationale consistently, but even if they were to do so, it would render the Scriptures unable to function in any sort of authoritative manner. Many elements of the Scriptures that seemed perfectly reasonable within seventh-, twelfth-, or seventeenth-century cultural paradigms are offensive today. Many that are acceptable today may become offensive tomorrow. Likewise, many that are offensive in the West are acceptable elsewhere, and vice versa. Rendering the contents of the Scriptures contingent on the knowledge and cultural attitudes of human authors and editors makes them little more than archaeological relics. While this view of the Scriptures may be acceptable within secular or atheistic approaches, it is inconsistent with how the Bible functions within the Church and therefore with the Christ who dwells there. Parceling out and relativizing the Word of God in this way prevents it from bearing authentic witness to Christ. Severed from the Holy Spirit, who inspired, preserves, and applies the Scriptures within the living Tradition of the Church, the Scriptures become dead letters.

Moreover, with one exception (2 Pet. 3:16), everything the New Testament proclaims regarding the Scriptures refers to the Old Testament. When St. Paul affirms that the Scriptures are breathed by God, the product of the Holy Spirit, he is talking about the Hebrew Scriptures (2 Tim. 3:16). When St. Peter says that men wrote as they were carried along by the Holy Spirit, he is referring to what would become the Christian Old Testament (2 Pet. 1:21). When St. Paul reiterates that Christ died and rose according to the Scriptures, he has in mind the Scriptures he inherited as a faithful Judean (1 Cor. 15:3–4). As St. Paul wrote his First Epistle to the Corinthians, none of the Gospels had been composed yet. One can approach the status of the Old Testament from the perspective of the authority of the apostolic testimony within the Church or from the perspective of accepting the authority of the New Testament. In either case, the result is the same: the experience of the Triune God found within the Hebrew Scriptures is authoritative for the Christian understanding of the identity of Christ.

There are some who marginalize only certain texts in the Old Testament—often Christians of a sort who refuse to completely dismiss the authority of the Hebrew Scriptures as an atheist or secularist might. Yet this view stumbles into another poor explanation for the problem of violence in the Old Testament. This generally takes the form of affirming the authority of the stories, prophecies, or poetic imagery of the Old Testament while simultaneously maintaining that they were not descriptions of actual historical events or phenomena. Even in the case of what may appear to be historical narrative, so the rationale goes, the narrated events likely never happened. The entire conquest of Canaan described in the Book of Joshua, for example, may be said to be an allegory for spiritual struggle, with the claim that no such battles ever took place.

Though this answer may appear less noxious to Christianity than the wholesale repudiation of scriptural authority, it nonetheless rests on the same problematic assumptions as the more secularist view described earlier. For example, there is no consistent methodological standard to delineate allegorical from literal or historical truths contained in Scripture. Critics sometimes marshal the lack of archaeological evidence for certain biblical events in support of this approach in order to marginalize the historical claims or data points in certain passages of the Scriptures. Yet this presumes, first, that the ancient text in question was originally intended to adhere to archaeological conditions or standards at some particular date.

Yet archaeology as a formalized discipline did not exist until fairly recently in human history. The kinds of archaeological reference points that would make sense to us today were not available to readers for most of the Bible's history and would not have been the benchmark used to deem one narrative figurative and another literal. Even now, constructions of the past based on archaeology are consistently subject to revision when new evidence is discovered. There is no distinction within the Scriptures themselves to indicate, for example, that the story of David and the giant Goliath is intended to be interpreted differently than the narration of David's taking of the city of Jerusalem or Omri's purchase of the hill that would become the site of Samaria. The status quo vis-a-vis the archaeological record of these three events has shifted during living memory.[4]

Compartmentalizing certain texts into ahistorical domains like parable or figurative expression is one thing; deeming them outright fiction is another. Not only does the latter compromise the authority of the Scriptures further; it risks conflating human attitudes with divine ones. This is particularly evident in how we understand depictions of violence in the Scriptures. No matter one's view of Scripture, no one would dispute the reality of violence and horror in the world, and it is reasonable to expect the Scriptures to offer at least some explanation for this painful truth. But suggesting that the violence described in the Scriptures is a parable or instructive allegory rather than a description of reality makes our view of God *more* rather than *less* problematic. If the Scriptures are not describing God's understanding of and response to actual episodes of genocide, murder, and rape, this would mean that He has chosen to reveal His character to humanity through fictional accounts of such atrocities. That the Scriptures contain such accounts can be explained only by their existence in reality. To argue otherwise would seem perverse, at least from any kind of theistic perspective.

---

4   Though barely mentioned in the Scriptures, Omri is well attested as a powerful king of the Northern Kingdom of Israel in the archaeological record and the textual remains of Israel's neighbors. The majority of scholars considered David to be a fictional founder of Israel until recent years in which inscriptions bearing his name were found, connecting him to Jerusalem. While scholars still consider the story of David and Goliath and the idea of giants in the ancient world to be fiction, recent finds in Philistine archaeology have already indicated that the name transliterated as "Goliath" is, in fact, a relatively common Philistine name.

While it is true that various Fathers and writers of the early Church spoke to the allegorical meanings of many Old Testament passages, it must be noted that none of them did so to deny or minimize the historical veracity of any biblical text. Quite the opposite: they consistently confirmed the historical content even when occasionally struggling with the moral message implied by the literal reading of the text. Moreover, allegory was introduced not at the level of interpretation but rather of application. The Fathers did not argue, for example, that certain texts were strictly allegorical or literary narrative and thus disconnected from historical reality. They sought not to transform or expunge a historical record, but rather to ensure that episodes of vengeance and violence not be repeated by their Christian hearers in the present through misguided application. Allegory is a useful tool to make relevant not only texts that, if applied literally, would present moral issues, but also texts that may seem simply irrelevant outside of their original historical milieu.

The revelation of Christ stands at the center of all the Scriptures. The Scriptures communicate Him to us, with His Father and His Spirit. Every encounter with Yahweh in the Scriptures inspires awe as well as penitence, which are not entirely comfortable states of being. They were not intended to bathe us in pure love and joy without also evoking awareness of our sinfulness. This is as true of Ss. Paul and John in the New Testament as it is of Moses and Isaiah in the Old. It should be expected that the commandments of God may cut our sinful flesh against the grain. It should be expected that the wisdom of God may confound our human foolishness. The Cross, an instrument of torture and violence, is foolishness to those who are perishing. But to those who are being saved, it is the wisdom and power of God (1 Cor. 1:18).

The God who reveals Himself in Scripture may at times seem to conflict with what seems right to us. But the ways of man lead to destruction. By sojourning through this tension, our views of ourselves, our lives, God, and His creation are reshaped and reformed in a way that is truly real. Wrestling with Christ as He appears to us in the Bible will yield His blessing only if we allow ourselves to be molded and taught. We cannot approach the Scriptures to find our own personal Jesus who conforms to who we may want, or even demand, that He be. Such a Jesus probably does not exist and so will avail us nothing. Rather, we must come to know the only Jesus Christ who does exist and through His grace offers to transform us into His likeness.

1

Divine Justice

MUCH OF THE VIOLENCE FOUND in the Scriptures is nested within language of justice, including language of punishment. In some cases, this violent justice comes at the hands of humans appointed to administer justice—judges and kings. In other cases, it is administered by God directly, as when Sodom and Gomorrah were consumed by fire or the plagues fell upon Egypt. Suffering, destruction, and death befall people in the world as a response to injustice or as motivated by the justice of God. These Old Testament images culminate in the series of disturbing scenes of darkness and doom that unfold in St. John's Revelation before the Last Judgment.

Divine justice is a central theme throughout the Scriptures. This is somewhat obscured in English translations, which rely on diverse words—among them *justice*, *righteousness*, *justification*, and *judge*—to translate what are, in fact, tightly related clusters of terms in both Hebrew and Greek. Further, the word *justice* itself has taken on a wide array of both positive and negative connotations. "Criminal justice" and "social justice," for example, are independent concepts that both interact with the concept of God's justice in diverse ways in contemporary theology. While a judge is seen as someone responsible for administering justice, the verb "to judge" has taken on a negative connotation of one person condemning another. This latter concept has also been applied to the concept of divine justice, specifically to Christ's Judgment of the living and the dead at His return. These associations have too often led to depriving God of any wrath or condemnation whatsoever in reaction.

In order to understand these interrelated themes within the Scriptures, the ancient understanding of justice must be recovered. The Psalter, for example, expresses the persistent hope that God will arise to judge the earth and scatter his enemies (Ps. 82/81:8; 68/67:1). Rather than contrasting God's justice with His mercy, as is now commonplace, His mercy and compassion are seen as the means by which He will eventually institute justice within His creation. God's establishment of justice is closely related to His identity as king. The justice of God, then, is also closely related to the foundations of human authority, rule, and kingship. The titles "Messiah" and "Christ," applied to Jesus in Hebrew and Greek respectively, identify Him as king. Yahweh, the God of Israel, from the time of Abraham, Isaac, and Jacob, has identified Himself with human people. Justice is a characteristic of this relationship between God and humanity and between humans and their neighbors. This has profound implications for the understanding of the Incarnation of Jesus Christ. One key purpose of God being made man is to restore these relationships of justice.

An old saying, variously attributed, says, "Justice, like lightning, ever should appear to few men's ruin but to all men's fear." Judgment should be feared by some, but not by all. For some, the establishment of justice is a future hope. This saying captures the connotation of divine justice in the Scriptures quite readily, as long as the "fear" spoken of is understood in the context of the fear of Yahweh, which is the beginning of wisdom (Prov. 9:10). The wise person is aware that justice will be established—meaning that justice is coming—and lives accordingly. This caution and insight are the fear and reverence required to approach the Creator of the universe. For those who willingly set themselves up as God's enemies, however, the prospect of judgment is one of terror and impending ruin. Much of the calamity that befalls people in the Scriptures occurs when God acts powerfully to restore justice.

The King's Justice

TODAY, JUSTICE CAN MEAN MANY different things. Likely the most prominent usage of the term is related to criminal justice, whose objective is to penalize criminals in proportion to their crimes. When offenders receive their due punishment, justice has been served. For a guilty person to go free or an innocent to be punished is injustice in the truest sense. In its ideal form, justice—often wearing a blindfold in artistic personifications—ought to be blind. It ought not take into account a person's relative wealth, rank, or station in life but permit only punishment that fits the crime in question. When meting out penalties and sentences, the criminal justice system considers many factors, including the intent to maximize deterrence, to minimize recidivism, and even to atone for the suffering caused by wrongdoing.

Criminal justice is commonly known as "retributive justice." The retribution is the punishment that is bestowed in response to the crime. Yet a second mode of justice, "distributive justice," is also a feature of the court system. Instead of simply punishing wrongdoers, distributive justice seeks restoration and restitution for victims. If one person has harmed someone or her property, distributive justice requires him to forfeit his own property to compensate for the damages. This is true in cases of both maliciousness and negligence. From the perspective of a perpetrator, distributive justice may be indistinguishable from retribution, as the perpetrator's suffered loss may be viewed as a punishment. From the perspective of the victim, however, it is aimed at a concrete alleviation of suffering rather than a simple appeal to a sense of justice or fairness.

More recently, growing attention has been paid to the need for "social justice." Rather than focusing on the isolated actions of individuals and their immediate consequences, social justice is concerned with the injustice at work in larger systems—communities, cultures, institutions, and nations. As imperfect human structures, oppressive habits and patterns tend to accrue in these societal systems, which benefit some while sabotaging others. If the guiding principles of these systems are tied to virtue, most communities will find them acceptable. If these structures are found, rather, to benefit or harm their members based on their race, nationality, gender, age, or socioeconomic status, for example, the structures themselves are considered unjust. Just as this sort of favoritism from one charged with enforcing the law would be unacceptable, so also is it unacceptable for this favoritism to be codified within the law itself or the functioning of the institutions that define and enforce it. These structures need to be examined and corrected to establish justice within and for the sake of the community.

All three forms of justice surface in the Torahic commandments of Scripture. Certain sins are considered particularly abominable: chiefly idolatry, sexual immorality, and murder. Thus the Law orders perpetrators of these crimes to be permanently removed from the community (e.g., Num. 15:30–31). Certain material objects generally used in these practices, such as pagan cultic objects, fall under the ban and must be destroyed (e.g., Deut. 7:25; 12:3). For most crimes and disputes within the community, the Torah calls for restitution from the perpetrator toward the victim. Thieves must repay what they have stolen (e.g., Ex. 22:1–4). Damaged or destroyed property must be replaced. Finally, specific commands seek to ensure that societal structures do not become oppressive. The Jubilee year requires the freeing of slaves and the restoration of lands to the families who originally owned them (Lev. 25:8–13). This command, if followed, would have prevented generational poverty and slavery.

Not only are examples of these three types of justice contained in the Hebrew Scriptures; the concept of justice throughout the Old Testament also encompasses all three. The Hebrew word generally translated as "justice" is *mishpat*,[1] which conveys a realm of space and time where all things exist in their proper place and relationship to one another. Deviations from this state constitute injustice. The commandments of the Torah are intended to prevent such injustices from occurring and also to prescribe correctives for when they do occur. To rectify these injustices and restore the state of justice is to judge (*shafat*).

God's justice is also one of the divine energies. God is just and is continuously working in His creation to bring about and preserve this state of justice. Therefore, for a human person or community to live in accordance with divine justice is to participate in His operation in creation. This participation is transformative and produces a state of blessing. "To bless," as a verb, is then to bring the person or thing blessed into alignment with God and His purposes in creation.

Likewise, for a human person or a human community to live in a way that is *un*just, that is, that runs against how God works within His created order, is to produce corruption. This rebellion is deformative and results in a state of curse. When someone or something is cursed, it is removed from the system of relationships that constitute justice in the world. So Cain, after committing murder, was cursed from the earth and no longer able to work the land to bring forth food through agriculture (Gen. 4:11–12). Throughout the Old Testament, curse entails banishment from the community and the place where God dwells.

In the ancient Near East, the cultural context from which the Scriptures emerge, the primary purpose and task of the king was to

---

1   This concept is roughly paralleled in other ancient Near Eastern contexts. For example, the Egyptian concept of *Ma'at* is functionally equivalent.

establish and maintain justice. For Israel's neighbors, this included harmony and peace with the gods, the spiritual beings who were seen to be a part of the human community through their special relationships with certain places and people groups. Kings were, therefore, also priests, up to and including the Roman emperor, who served as *pontifex maximus*, or high priest, of the pagan sacrificial rites. Sacrifices that kings, other leaders, and heads of families offered were communal meals aimed at uniting inhabitants of the community with one another and with their gods. For this reason, the king himself was seen to be divine and, therefore, able to bridge the visible and invisible worlds.

This role of the pharoah, for example, is the subtext of the ten plagues God unleashed on Egypt (Ex. 7—12). The Book of Exodus portrays the plagues as a battle between Yahweh and the gods of Egypt, who had been complicit in the enslavement and abuse of the Hebrew people, not to mention countless other injustices. Therefore, Yahweh's defeat of these gods is their judgment (Ex. 12:12). Throughout this judgment, however, Pharaoh acts as interlocutor, bridging and acting on behalf of the mutually complicit human community and that of the gods. The Egyptian people expected their king to restore justice and peace in the face of plague and curse, but he is utterly unable to. His scribal priests, the "magicians" of English translations, are incapable of assisting him, even as expert intermediaries with the spiritual world in general and the gods in particular (Ex. 7:10–12, 22; 8:7, 18).

Within Israel, the relationships between Yahweh and the high priest—and the kings who came later—were different. In terms of chronology, the first leader of Israel was Moses, succeeded by Joshua, then the judges, and finally the kings. Their task was not to mollify or manipulate God but rather, as His servant and image, to establish His justice in Israel. This is why the judges of the Old Testament were known by that title, although they did not hear trials or cases.

Throughout the Book of Judges, through rebellion and injustice, Israel and her various tribal units brought down a curse upon themselves, which typically manifested itself as foreign domination. God then raised up a judge in response to their repentance to reestablish justice in the land.

While the Israelite leadership—including the king—sought to establish justice by galvanizing obedience to the commandments, the priesthood brought about justice by means of ritual, typically through the rites of repentance and atonement. These purification rites staved off the curse and exile that would otherwise result from allowing sin and injustice to fester within the community. The priesthood also confirmed and strengthened the relationships of Israelites to one another and to God. The ritual life of the tabernacle and temple both furthered the ties of justice and rectified injustice. The offerings of thanksgiving formed the core of the daily sacrificial rites related to the offering of incense and other offerings. These rites served to bring worshippers more deeply into positive participation in God's operations within His creation, including His justice.

The state of justice, then, is the original state of the created order. In fact, it is the order that constitutes God's creative act against chaos. The lasting rest and peace of the age to come, an age without end, will be ordered by divine justice. Sin, suffering, and death in this age are the result of violating this order in creation. The order found within creation is the product of the ongoing creative activity of God. To oppose this order, or even to attack it, is to rebel against the Creator and seek to work at cross purposes. Like attempts to resist the flow of a rushing river, opposition to the mighty working of God results in destruction.

As the divine king, Christ is the minister of this justice, the one who judges (John 5:22). Christ is not only the son of David and therefore the king of Israel; He is also God the Son. Christ's eternal rule is the fulfillment of what was only a partial and fallible relationship in the Old Testament between God and the king. In the Person of Jesus Christ, the throne of Yahweh and the throne of David are united. His reign is one of both threat and promise. Unlike a fallible human king, Christ establishes eternal and perfect justice, which will one day expand to fill the entirety of creation.

Father of the Fatherless and Protector of Widows

THE TASK OF A JUDGE, then, in rendering judgment or judging, whether in a court context or the context of the Book of Judges, is to establish or restore justice. Therefore, when Yahweh condemns the leadership of Israel and Judah, a chief charge is that they have judged unjustly (e.g., Is. 10:1). To judge unjustly is to show favoritism, to create laws that are oppressive and do harm, or to ignore injustice rather than righting it. Yahweh, in the Old Testament, contrasts Himself to this kind of judge, the human judges with whom the people are familiar. Yahweh does not respect persons and will not accept bribes (Deut. 10:17). It is in reflection of His character and their own responsibility to execute His justice that God forbids the judges of Israel to take bribes or to show favoritism (Deut. 10:19).

This is not to say, however, that the Scriptures present Yahweh as nonpartisan. God associates Himself with some and opposes others. Typically, when the Hebrew Scriptures condemn favoritism, it is not a general prohibition but rather a specific judgment against accepting bribes.[2] The Scriptures do not condemn the poor and destitute, since they are not usually prone to offering bribes. Neither does God condemn the favoritism of a judge taking a side in the administration of justice, but rather a judge who sides with the wealthy and

---

2   See, for example, Ex. 18:21; 23:8; Deut. 27:25; 1 Sam. 8:3; 2 Chron. 19:7; Job 6:22; 15:34; Ps. 15/14:5; 26/25:10; Prov. 15:27; 17:8, 23; Eccl. 7:7; Is. 1:23; 5:23; 33:15; Ezek. 22:12; Amos 5:12; Mic. 3:11; 7:3.

powerful for personal gain. This condemnation of favoritism toward the wealthy is echoed in the New Testament (James 2:1–9).

It is impossible to establish or restore justice without taking a side or, perhaps more appropriately, taking up a cause. In particular, justice requires taking up the cause of the victims of injustice. It requires setting one's self against the perpetrators of the injustice in question. This kind of stance will naturally favor victims and call for action against their oppressors—action that the Scriptures always refer to as a punishment for their crimes, whether it takes the form of restitution, exile, or even the death penalty. In the Scriptures, reflecting the milieu of the ancient Near East, the archetypal social categories of the weak and oppressed are orphans and widows (Job 22:9; Is. 10:2; Jer. 49:11; Ezek. 22:25; Mark 12:40; James 1:27). Yahweh is the "Father of the fatherless and protector of widows" (Ps. 68/67:5).

It is not a violation of God's impartiality for Him to take the side of the powerless against the powerful but rather a consequence of it. The two are cited in the same breath:

> For Yahweh, your God, is God of gods and Lord of lords. He is the great, the mighty, and the fearsome God. He it is who is not partial and takes no bribe. He executes justice for the orphan and the widow. He loves the stranger, giving to him food and clothing. Love the stranger, then, because you were strangers in the land of Egypt. You will fear Yahweh your God. You will serve Him and cling to Him. By His name, you shall swear. He is your praise. He is your God, who has done for you these great and terrifying things that you have seen with your own eyes. Your fathers went down to Egypt with seventy people. Now Yahweh your God has made you like the stars of heaven in number. (Deut. 10:17–19)

In the Torah, Yahweh commands Israel to establish and maintain justice based on His own justice, thereby participating in His action in creation. He reinforces this by pointing to the fact that the Israelites themselves have been recipients of this same favor. Yahweh allied Himself with the Hebrews, the descendants of Abraham, when they were slaves in a foreign land and powerless. He then wrought a terrible vengeance on Egypt and her gods on nascent Israel's behalf to give her justice.

Pharaoh greeted the initial approach of Moses and Aaron with derision for precisely this reason. What concern to him were the threats of a god of slaves? There is a sharp contrast here with the gods of the nations. Basic to ancient ritual was the idea that the worship of a divine being made one more like that being. Thus, the pagan nations worshipped gods of power, beauty, victory in war, sexual prowess, fertility, health, strength, and speed. There were no gods of weakness, victimhood, defeat, infertility, or sickness. Or if there were such spirits, at the very least no pagan would worship them but instead would attempt to ward them off.

Yahweh, the God of Israel, however, is not the embodiment of human virtue or desire, nor is He the offerer of one particular good or virtue as opposed to others. Rather, He is the Creator and the Judge of all the earth. Justice, or righteousness,[3] is not simply a quality of personal excellence. Judgment is a divine action within creation that continuously moves and drives all created things to form, uphold, and restore the created order. He is, therefore, the avenger of the orphan and the widow while He opposes the proud.

It is, then, no surprise that when the God of Israel became incarnate, He was not born the son of the emperor or even into the Herodian dynasty. In taking upon Himself our shared human nature, Christ continued to identify with the weak, the poor, and the oppressed. He was born to a young mother under circumstances that

---

3   The same Greek word is translated as both "justice" and "righteousness" in English translations of the Scriptures in various contexts.

rendered Him subject to suspicion (John 8:41). He was born into a Galilean peasant family in a village so small it likely moved with the seasons. Saint Joseph, as a day laborer, did what would today be considered "handyman" work for fellow peasants to survive. Lacking the status of Roman citizens, Jesus and His family were legally categorized as *non persona*. He spent His adult life essentially homeless and dependent on the hospitality of others. He ended His life falsely convicted, dying the most humiliating and torturous death that a tyrannical government could devise.

An oft-neglected emphasis in the New Testament authors' explanation of Christ's Resurrection is justification in the sense of vindication (Rom. 4:25). There is good evidence, however, that vindication was a major theme in apostolic preaching (e.g., Acts 2:36; 5:30–31). Though Jesus had been condemned and executed as a criminal and false Messiah, His Father vindicated Him, revealing Him to be the Christ by raising Him from the dead. Throughout the Hebrew Scriptures, Israel's God identifies with the powerless and the poor. Throughout the Hebrew Scriptures, He promises them not only healing and restoration but also justice. He promises that the day will come when He will once again order the world aright, vindicating His people and lifting them up while those who have oppressed them, profited from their misery, and done them harm will be laid low. Christ's Resurrection is the beginning of the fulfillment of that promise.

The Last Judgment

WHILE CHRIST'S RESURRECTION IS THE beginning of God's reestablishment of justice in the creation, it is the general resurrection, the resurrection of all the dead, that the Scriptures speak of together with the Last Judgment. This is, in fact, the reason that this event is referred to as the Last Judgment. Judgment, again, is not the issuing of a criminal verdict, as if there had been a series of such verdicts issued provisionally, and this is the last one. Rather, judgment is the restoration of justice, of the correct order, and harmony of creation. The Last Judgment, then, at Christ's glorious appearing, represents the fulfillment, the final conclusion, of Yahweh's restoration of justice to the world. At this point, its results will become final.

Because sin violates and corrupts the created order and its justice, it has consequences within creation. Corruption produces strife, discord, and death. Corruption gives a foothold within the creation to spiritual powers hostile to humanity. Without the intervention of God to establish justice through judgment, the creation would quickly sink into chaos, violence, and destruction, as occurred before the Flood of Noah (Gen. 6:5). One of God's eternal activities in His creation is the ongoing restraint of these evil forces brought down upon humanity by people's sins.

Often, Christians of the present day discuss the "problem of evil." Why does a good, loving, and all-powerful God allow evil in the world? Perhaps this question itself is misguided or based on a false premise. Not only does it presume humanity is the innocent victim of evil, but also that evil is an external force from which, it is imagined, God is failing to protect us. The reality is precisely the reverse—evil enters creation as a result of humanity's collusion with evil spiritual forces. Humanity is the vehicle through which evil comes into the world, and it is most often directly inflicted by humans upon one another rather than by impersonal forces of nature. God's merciful and gracious action is why this evil does not consume the creation entirely.

Nevertheless, God does allow the consequences of sin and corruption to at least partially play out in His creation. What is often labeled as God's judgment, wrath, or punishment is really His allowing the perpetrators of iniquity to experience the full consequences of their sin. As always, this judgment is not punitive, though we may experience it as the punishment or the price of sin. Rather, to truly restore justice and order requires either repentance of the sin and evil that have disrupted the good order of creation or the removal of the unrepentant sinner.

Within the Book of Judges, the people of Israel repeatedly fell into sin and wickedness. In response, God withdrew His protective hand and allowed disunited, weak, and struggling Israel to fall under the oppression of wicked nations. Under this oppression, Israel would cry out to God for deliverance (Judg. 3:9, 15; 4:3; 6:7; 10:10–12), who would then raise up a judge, a leader through whom, often despite his personal failings, God would reestablish justice. But in the process, at least for a time, Israel, having been chastised, would be chastened.

Had God merely continued to restrain the consequences of the sin of Israel, that evil would have continued to deepen and worsen. This would mean, in concrete terms, that more of God's people, whom He loves, would have been victimized and with more horrible outcomes. One solution would be simply to slay all the wicked. But the God of Israel loves humanity, and not one human person remains utterly untouched by sin. He loves not only the unquestionably innocent but also the perpetrators of evil (Ezek. 18:23, 32; 33:11; 2 Pet. 3:9).

In various circumstances, every human is both the committer of sin and its victim. For this reason, even when God gives sinful humanity over to the consequences of their sin, they are measured and aimed at repentance and restoration (Rom. 11:32). This process continues until unrepentant evil reaches a point at which tolerating it further would not be mercy for the perpetrator but a failure of mercy for the ongoing victims. The Revelation of St. John depicts the complete unleashing of the powers of evil in response to human sin before the Day of Judgment arrives. God finally withdraws His restraining hand, as the purpose of that restraint is at an end.

The Final Judgment at Christ's glorious appearing thus represents the end of this cycle and the end of the period of mercy for the offender in favor of ultimate and eternal mercy for the wronged.

Perfect justice will be established eternally at that very point. Perfect justice in the created order requires action with regard to humanity. Humanity must also be judged in order to enter into the life of the age to come. Because all of humanity has been touched by sin and is thus tainted by the curse, human persons who are going to enter into the Kingdom must be justified. This is not so much a legal declaration of innocence (they are not innocent), but rather it signifies justification in the truest sense, of being set aright, of being restored to order as people and even as an entire cosmic creation.

Justification takes place through repentance and the forgiveness of sins. The former represents actual human effort. Repentance is not only sorrow for sins, but concrete action to struggle against sin and to heal the damage inflicted by sin upon the sinner and the victims of that sin. Forgiveness is not merely God setting aside wrath or prospective punishments. Forgiveness is actual healing, restoration, and setting the human person back into order. This is why baptism has always been understood in terms of justification.[4] Baptism is "of repentance" and "for the remission of sins" (Acts 2:38). A person enters into baptism repentantly and receives the remission of sins. Later acts of repentance and forgiveness are seen as a renewal of baptism and therefore signify an ongoing justification of the human person. The Christian life is one of continual repentance in preparation for the coming Day of Judgment. Those who refuse repentance and justification until the end leave only one possibility for their fate. They must be removed from the created order entirely so that it can be set in order, an ordering they refuse.

In the days of Noah, humanity in its utter depravity corrupted the entire creation with violence and chaos. God responded by purifying the created order of humanity entirely (Gen. 6:5–7). After the Flood,

---

4   As in the Orthodox baptismal service, "Thou art justified, thou art illumined, thou art washed."

God set down His bow and declared peace with humanity, promising never again to destroy mankind. Instead, He makes provision for the purification of repentant humanity through forgiveness (9:12–17). The judgment that justifies human persons, baptism, still takes the form of water, as did the Flood (1 Pet. 3:19–21). Our God is a consuming fire (Heb. 12:29). That fire will be poured forth on the Day of Judgment (Is. 66:16; 1 Cor. 3:13–15; 1 Pet. 4:12; 2 Pet. 3:7–12). This fire will either consume our sin or consume us with our sin, based on our repentance (Is. 4:4; Zech. 13:9; Heb. 10:27). The healing of human justification is not a placid or passive event but one that involves suffering, discipline, struggle, and effort. All these human efforts, however, are participations in the work of God to heal, discipline, judge, and transform His human creation, along with all of His creation, into the transfigured beauty of the age to come (Phil. 2:12–13).

2

The Nature
of Death

D EATH IS AN EVIL. SAINT Paul describes it as the last enemy (1 Cor. 15:26), which has been defeated by Christ in His Resurrection and will be put to an end at His glorious appearing. Death is the result of sin (Rom. 5:12; 6:23). The violence found in Scripture, at least of the variety that is considered problematic, chiefly takes the form of human death. Unlike the laws of surrounding nations, the Torah does not penalize sin by means of torture or deliberately inflicting suffering. Likewise, sexual violence is strictly proscribed as wickedness. Nonetheless, there is certainly no shortage of killing in Scripture. Despite strict prohibitions on various forms of murder and manslaughter, God Himself takes human lives. He further commands humans to take other human lives, sometimes *en masse*. Within these killings, within and outside of war, children and other innocents lose their lives.

The problem here is obvious. Were it not for human rebellion and sin, there would be no death. Death was not part of God's good creation at its beginning. Christ's great victory results in its destruction. It is evil, so how can the same good God command it? The answer, once again, is not to seek to explain away or otherwise neutralize the Scriptures. Nor is it to argue that death is somehow not an evil and thereby deform the gospel. Rather, the answer is found in the elaboration of a more full-orbed understanding of death and, through this, of the present life of humans in this world.

At the expulsion from Paradise in Genesis 3, God does not issue death as a punishment, a "death penalty." Adam and Eve do not fall down dead on the spot because of their sin. Rather, they are cut off from life and banished into this present world. This is a direct act of God that results in death. He therefore uses death, the result of sin, for His own purposes. Once we understand the role death plays within the divine economy and the life of a human person, God's utilization of death in the Scriptures becomes intelligible.

It Is Not Good That Man Should Live Forever

DEATH COMES TO HUMANITY IN the third chapter of Genesis. This portion of the Genesis text has taken on outsized importance in the Christian theology of the West, primarily through the work of St. Augustine. The first eleven chapters of Genesis describe numerous instances of human cooperation in spiritual rebellion, and the expulsion from Paradise is critical among them. It was also commonplace for various Fathers, notably St. Augustine, to focus on one of these instances as paradigmatic. The near-total focus on the "fall of Adam" in the West, however, has led to both a lack of familiarity with the other episodes of human rebellion in Genesis and a misunderstanding of Paradise and exile.

The standard Western treatment of Genesis 3 revolves around Adam as the first sinner who receives the death penalty as the result of his transgression of God's commandment. But within the text, it is Cain in Genesis 4 who is seen as the archetypal sinner, not Adam. Likewise, there is not a hint in the text itself that death is a judicially imposed penalty. God does not describe death to Adam in terms of retributive justice, either before or after he eats from the tree of the knowledge of good and evil. He is told that in the day in which he eats of it, he will die—not that he will be killed (Gen. 2:16–17).

Genesis actually describes death not as a punishment from God but for a purpose that is ultimately to man's benefit. In Genesis 3:22–24, God states to the angelic beings surrounding the throne that through the knowledge of good and evil, humanity has become like one of them (v. 22). It is not good that man should live forever in that state, and therefore God takes the action of driving humanity out of Paradise and placing a cherubim with a flaming sword to guard against reentry (vv. 23–24). That man should live forever in the presence of God is, of course, good. Eternal life is the product of the salvation achieved by Christ. A never-ending life in this world, with all its suffering, sickness, evil, and violence, however, would be hell on earth. Created but immortal evil beings already existed before Adam's transgression. The devil, who was cursed just before this proclamation, is one example (vv. 14–15). Were humanity to live forever in that state, we would have become like the demons and remain forever mired in evil and rebellion.

This action of exile results in human death, and it is the solution to the problem of humanity living forever in the state brought about by eating from the tree. In what sense have Adam and his wife become like angelic beings? They have not gained new knowledge of the good. Before eating, good was all that they knew, because God had created all things good. Rather, humanity had gained the knowledge of evil. This knowledge is not just an intellectual idea or thought but intimate knowledge. Evil had now become part of humanity's being and future possibilities. Understanding the depths of evil makes good—namely God Himself—more difficult to know. Being acquainted with evil creates the temptation to view its simple negation as good in itself. Since the expulsion from Paradise, humans have constantly faced the

31

temptation to view created goods, the good things of this world, as the ultimate good to be pursued.

Again, God does not slay Adam or do him any direct harm. Rather, He makes for him and his wife garments of flesh and cuts them off from the Tree of Life at the center of Paradise. God is the source of life. Being cut off from God through exile from His presence is a kind of death in and of itself—spiritual death. In addition, this spiritual death, over time, brings about physical death and the departure of the soul, the life, from the body. Neither of these deaths is the cessation of existence. Rather, life itself, dwelling with God eternally, is replaced with another mode of life characterized by suffering and difficulty that ends in physical death.

Cherubim, as they appear in Scripture, are heavenly beings also described in Babylonian religious traditions. They are spiritual beings that protect divine thrones. The expulsion of humanity from the presence of God was not merely a punishment of rejection. It was also required to protect sinful and rebellious humanity from the presence of God and His holiness, which had become dangerous to them. Further redemptive action would be required for humanity to be able to reenter God's presence safely and experience eternal life with Him.

As a result of our first parents' rebellion, humanity, at least for a time, lost something. Humanity lost the ability to live in the joy and peace of the presence of God and share in His eternal divine life. The Scriptures then unfold the story of the battle waged by God to bring humanity back to this purpose for which they were created. In addition to this at least temporary loss, humanity was given this life, in this world, with all its joys and sorrows. This mortal life is one of change and inconstancy. The capacity for growth and change makes possible both repentance and maturity, on one hand, and corruption and destruction on the other. While the loss of the life of which God is the source may be permanent, the life given to us by God in this world means that it does not have to be.

Human life in this world, in this age, has repentance and growth to spiritual maturity as its purpose. It is, therefore, not an end in itself. Long life in this world is not necessarily something to be prized if it is a life of pain, suffering, and degradation. A short life in this world is not necessarily a curse or a loss if that short time completes in a person what many longer-lived people fail to receive (WSol 4:13). Scripture portrays God's removal of Enoch from the increasingly dark and violent world that preceded Noah's Flood as a positive, as his removal from further pain and suffering (4:10–15). This language of being "chosen" and "taken" is used repeatedly to describe departed Christians within the Orthodox funeral services.

A world populated by immortal demons would literally be hell. Physical death brings an end to both evil and suffering. For those who work evil, it brings the suffering and violence they are able to inflict to an end. For the victims of that same evil, it brings to an end their suffering and victimhood. At the time of Noah's Flood, Yahweh is portrayed as further limiting the life of humanity (Gen. 6:3). Physical death, specifically human mortality, like justice, is, therefore, a threat to some to bring about repentance and to others a promise of relief and salvation. Though it is an evil and a consequence of sin, the Creator uses physical death as the end of life in this world to bring about man's good and the possibility of restoration and eternal life.

It Is Appointed to Man Once to Die

THE EPISTLE TO THE HEBREWS states that it is appointed to man once to die, and after this comes the judgment (9:27). Death represents not only the end of evil and sin but also the point at which justice is reestablished, no matter how greatly unjust the circumstances of a person's life may have been. For the duration of a single human life, the wicked may have prospered, or the innocent may have suffered horrible injustices. The life of a human person may have been tragically short and filled with terrible pain. It may have been incredibly long and filled with sin and debauched pleasures. Both of these violations of the justice built into God's creation are resolved at death.

Mortal life in this world, in this age, is given by God for a particular purpose of repentance, as already described. The end of this present life in death, then, is the conclusion of that process of repentance and transformation or the end of the opportunity for the same. Because of what comes after, a short, innocent, virtuous life in this age, filled as it is with violence and wickedness, is no punishment. Likewise, a long life of unrepentant wickedness is no blessing but a foretaste of the perdition that follows. As St. Paul writes, the present sufferings of this life are not worthy of comparison to the richness of blessings that await the faithful in the age to come (Rom. 8:18).

Many moral criticisms of the Old Testament proceed from a materialist vantage point. We assume that this temporal life is all there is for human existence. Therefore, any death or killing of a human that is depicted—or worse, *ordered* by God—in Scripture is the ultimate evil. If the children of giant clans and other tribes are killed, they die as innocent victims, not guilty of their parents' abhorrent behavior. It may be accepted that at a certain point, perpetrators of unspeakable wickedness must die to put an end to their evil, but how would their children be anything but innocent victims receiving punishment from God for the sin of their fathers?

These materialist presuppositions, however, are not the paradigm(s) at work in the Scriptures themselves. These events, these killings, are conveyed within an overarching context and thus must be assessed morally within that framework. This framework largely understands this life as a time of opportunity for repentance, rife as it is with suffering, after which we either go on to eternal life in the presence of our Creator or remain eternally condemned. Within this framework, the member of the giant clan engaged actively in atrocities has wasted his opportunity for repentance, healing, and transformation (Ezek. 18:23, 32; 33:11). If his child's life is lost in the process, that child is not the victim of injustice before God's own judgment seat but is spared a life of suffering, pain, and potentially following his or her parents and culture into wickedness and destruction.

Throughout the Old Testament, God is the judge of when and how a person will end life. Lives are saved and preserved at the will of God in situations impossible to survive, from fiery furnaces and lions' dens to unwinnable battles in war. Likewise, vastly superior military forces meet their end in the Red Sea or encamped around Jerusalem. It is God, the Creator and Judge of all, who determines when repentance and purification are sufficient for His children to come into His presence and share in His eternal divine life. It is God, the Creator and Judge of all, who determines when the opportunities for repentance for a person have reached their end, balanced against their future wickedness. God protects the weak and innocent from others and from themselves. God also protects future victims from those who would harm them through administering justice in the form of death.

Holding this understanding of death, there is more to be said about the death penalties prescribed by the Torah for various crimes. While there are still many Christians who see the death penalty as appropriate in cases of murder or other very specific crimes, relatively few would argue for its application in cases of, for example, disrespect to parents or the fraud of a woman being found not to be a virgin on her wedding night. This gives rhetorical power to the non-Christian objector, who states that mandating the death penalty for such offenses is therefore immoral.

The fact that Christians do not embrace a literal application of these commandments from the Torah is also often used as an argument to relativize the seriousness of other sins that required the death penalty in a literal reading. It is sometimes argued in response that the prescribed death penalty is merely a categorization of these as "mortal sins" or "sins unto death." We must admit that saying that a sin is very serious is a far cry from saying that it is worthy of death. In any case, the composers of the Torah understood that sins had different degrees of severity, yet this did not necessarily translate to imposing some kind of death penalty for the most destructive sins.

In order to understand why the Torah would require death for these various transgressions, one must first recognize how the Torah itself views life and death. Our modern perspective is highly oriented toward the individual, and we naturally read the commandments of the Torah in this way. The Torah's self-understanding, however, relates these commandments to the community viewed as a whole, not a collection of individuals.

The theme of life and death begins in the opening chapters of Genesis. In our modern era, so much of our discussion has concerned the historicity of the various narratives in the Book of Genesis that we are prone to lose sight of its place in the Torah. In its canonical form, Genesis is not an independent text but rather serves as the historical and theological prologue to the Torah as a whole. The major themes of the later commandments and ritual instructions are found initially in Genesis, and Genesis should shape the understanding of the events and teachings related in Exodus through Deuteronomy.

Life, in Paradise, was to eat from the Tree of Life and thereby to remain forever in the presence of God, sharing His life. On the day that our first parents chose to eat from the tree of the knowledge of good and evil, they died in being cut off from the Tree of Life and expelled from the place of God's presence. Throughout the Torah, this is the understanding of what life and death mean, including biological life and death. The living God dwells in the land of the living, and the slain who lie in the grave are cut off from his life-giving hand (Ps. 88/87:5). Here the ideas of death and exile are brought together and united.

Later, in the commandments of the Torah, the common phrase is that certain sins require that a person be "cut off from among the people" (e.g., Num. 15:30–31). It is ambiguous whether this refers to expulsion from the community or a literal death penalty, not because of our lack of historical knowledge but precisely because both of these ideas are so closely united in the vision of the text. When the place where God is becomes the camp with the tabernacle at the center, and still later when it becomes the kingdom with the temple at its theological center, to be expelled or cut off from that place, and God's presence, is death. The situation continues and is the subject of meditation in the post exilic psalms and prophets.

It is also important to note that the status of being cut off from among the people and from the presence of God was not beyond repair. The entire system of sin and guilt offerings for purification allowed for sinful people to remain in, or reenter, the place of God's presence. Discussion of the "law" and its penalties often leaves aside the fact that the Torah includes concrete means of repentance and restoration. The Torah as a whole is not merely a means of governance for Israel. It represents the expression of what is now required of Israel, now that God is dwelling among them, and the means of restoring justice, the right relation of things, after a disruption. Numbers 15 explicitly ties cutting off a person from the community to their lack of repentance, in addition to the nature of their sin. When sin enters the community through a person, this can be remedied either by the person's repentance or by the removal of that person from the community.

Saint Paul applies this part of the Law quite directly in 1 Corinthians 5:1–13. A man in Corinth is guilty of gross sexual immorality within his own family, which under the Torah requires him to be cut off from among the people. The church in Corinth has done nothing about it. Saint Paul points out that this situation cannot be allowed to stand. The man must be removed from the community. But even in this extreme case, St. Paul extends the idea that this will hopefully work toward the man's repentance and salvation. Excommunication from the church community is the direct equivalent of exile from the Old Covenant community and is the remedy for unrepentant sin throughout the New Testament (see Matt. 18:17; 2 Thess. 3:6; 1 Tim. 1:20).

In addition to being expelled from the place where Christ dwells, excommunication means that one is excluded from eating from the Tree of Life. Eating of that tree is fulfilled in the Eucharist as the ongoing source of life in the Kingdom of God (John 6:53–57). Far from being a "watering down" of the judicial penalties of the Torah, excommunication from the church community, as taught by the apostles and practiced by the Church through the centuries, is a direct and literal application of the principles, and the penalties, of the Torah. As the salvation and life found in Christ are greater than the ordinances and community of the Old Covenant, so also is the peril of being cut off from Christ and His Church greater than the peril of being cut off from Israel of old.

The taking of human life as an act of judgment, then, occurs in different contexts across the Old Testament. Israel administers death judicially in cases of particular sins that cannot be allowed to continue within the community. God orders death against tribes, clans, and nations whose wickedness and oppression can no longer be allowed to continue. In all these cases, death must be understood in this twofold manner. Death is an act of judgment that cuts off the further wickedness and evil of the oppressor while protecting, finally and eternally, the victims of sin and evil. Death is also exile, to be cut off from life, and can thereby serve a remedial purpose. The destruction of our sinful flesh not only allows but brings about the salvation of our souls (1 Cor. 5:5).

Swallowed Up in Victory

THE EPISTLE TO THE HEBREWS describes the devil as the one who wields the power of death (2:14). The devil received this dominion over the dead in the curse that was laid upon him for his part in the exile of humanity from Paradise (Gen. 3:14). Ancient people were fully aware that serpents ate small rodents and other animals, not dirt. Rather, the dust eaten by the devil is the dust from which Adam had been made and to which he would return (v. 19). For this reason, the devil and Hades frequently appear in Christian iconography as a serpent or a gaping maw swallowing up the dead.

As with all the rebellious spiritual powers, God uses even the devil's spite and hatred of humanity to bring about good. As has been discussed, God does this with the evil of death itself. The devil was given his limited domain not by some compulsion placed on God but with a purpose and for a period of time. In the New Testament, the ferocity of the devil in opposing the Church of Christ is based on his knowledge that his time, that brief time given him by God, is coming to an end (e.g., 1 Pet. 5:8; Rev. 12:12). Death, as it finishes its purpose, is being abolished.

The gospel is the report of the victory of God achieved by Jesus Christ over the hostile spiritual powers arrayed against humanity. Central to that proclamation is Christ's Resurrection from the dead. Central to the understanding of Christ's Resurrection is the event of the harrowing of Hades. This is portrayed by the Scriptures not only as the defeat of the devil and the exodus of the righteous dead to Paradise from Hades, but also as the defeat of death itself (e.g., 1 Cor. 15:54–57). The idea of the destruction of death and the defeat of the devil go hand in hand with understanding the death and Resurrection of Christ (Heb. 2:14).

Christ's conquest of death results in His authority and lordship over the living and the dead (Acts 10:42; 2 Tim. 4:1; 1 Pet. 4:5). This gives Christ the authority to judge all of humanity, return humanity to its proper estate, and give us our destiny. Those who have spent this life seeking salvation through repentance and transformation will spend eternity sharing in the divine life of the Holy Trinity, the purpose for which humanity was created. Those who have failed to do so will receive the destiny proper to them from the time of Adam's expulsion from Paradise, the same fate faced by the devil and his angels.

Christ redeems all of humanity from death. The resurrection of the dead is universal (John 5:25–28). All those who have lived will live again and stand before the judgment seat of Christ. Salvation and life, however, are not universal (v. 29). The Orthodox iconography of the Resurrection and the harrowing of Hades depict the resurrection of Adam and Eve and, through these first parents, all of humanity. Orthodox iconography does not depict the resurrection and salvation of Cain, the archetypal sinner, nor of Judas or other sons of perdition. God uses death for particular purposes then abolishes it.

Sin, evil, and wickedness are not from God. He restrains, limits, and restricts them. He removes, purifies, and heals them. But those who cling to their sins and wickedness without repentance perish with them. The ritual aspects of the "death penalties" of the Torah and the rest of the Old Testament were the community's participation in the reality of the Last Judgment. Likewise, St. Paul understands the process of church discipline, including excommunication, as just such a preparation. The apostle urges the community at Corinth in the case of an unrepentantly sinful man to "hand this man over to Satan for the destruction of the flesh, so that his spirit might be saved on the day of the Lord" (1 Cor. 5:5; see also 1 Tim. 1:20). These commandments are not about violence, destruction, wrath, or revenge. Rather, they are a call to repentance. They are a call to return to the central and primary purpose of this life. They are a preparation for the life of the world to come.

CHAPTER

3

Sin as
Infection

B OTH WITHIN AND OUTSIDE THE Christian faith, the word
"sin" is most often used to refer to a specific action that is judged
to be morally wrong. Sins are a function of freewill decisions made
by individual people who can choose to do good or evil. However,
defining sin in this way makes the various measures undertaken in
the Old Testament to control and purify sin difficult to understand.
When violent actions are taken against humans or animals in pursuit of this moral purity, those actions seem unjustified or even cruel.
Modern commentators often describe Israel's sacrificial system solely
in terms of violence committed against animals.

Beginning with Cain, however, the Hebrew Scriptures present sin
in a very different way. Sin is portrayed as a force, sometimes even
as a demonic creature, that Adam's transgression released into the
world. Sin is less a judgment cast upon an action than a poison or a
deadly disease. Individual evil actions are symptoms of this disease
that reveal its presence and the degree of its progression toward
death. Sin can pass from one person to another. Sin can intensify

within a population and become a defining aspect of a community. Like a virus or bacteria in our modern understanding, sin leaves its mark and its contagion in the world. This stain left by sin poisons not only humans but animals, plants, and even the inanimate objects of God's created order. Thus the Torah prescribes actions that are aimed at containing and eliminating the disease of sin. Purification was a battle with life-and-death stakes.

Despite this, it has become commonplace in religious contexts to understand sin in juridical terms, namely in terms of crime and punishment. In this view, God's law essentially functions as a list of rules. Breaking any one of them is a sin—a crime of greater or lesser severity—that God is honor-bound to punish out of His just nature. The antidote to the problem of sin, as understood in this framework, is simply not to break the rules. Repentance quickly becomes little more than the means of bypassing punishment for one's crime(s).

But the idea of divine judgment as a punishment for sin-as-crime raises questions that are difficult to reconcile with traditional Christian understandings of the relationship between God and humanity. First, if divine judgment is punitive, it is worthy to wonder whether the punishments God issues actually fit the crimes committed by humans. The elephant in the room, of course, is hell, typically conceived of as the ultimate, eternal punishment for sin. Is this a fair penalty? Further, the entire nature of God and His rules becomes dubious. Are His laws based on some eternal concept of justice that compels Him (despite His supposed omnipotence) to certain actions? Must every sin be punished? Are these laws built into nature? If so, is this because God has written them in nature, or are they a necessary by-product of His creative act? Are these laws founded purely in God's will? Is a thought or an action sinful merely because God has said so? If so, does God directly commanding what would otherwise be a sin, as when Abraham was commanded to sacrifice his son, make it not sinful in that particular case?

Rather than providing an interpretive grid that gives insight into the way sin and judgment function in the Scriptures, the juridical framework merely opens up an ever more complex web of questions that have long served as fodder of debate within Western Christianity.

The issue becomes even more complicated when the concept of "guilt" is brought into the picture. When considering guilt in a criminal court, the judge considers a number of mitigating factors before meting out punishment. In the Scriptures, God judges whole nations collectively for sin. It's unlikely that every individual who suffered or died under these judgments was equally complicit in the nation's sins. Indeed, the sins committed by the powerful—the leaders of these communities—often results in judgment upon tribes, clans, cities, and nations. Yet the judgment strikes many who seem innocent, including children. Here there is no direct correlation between the degree of suffering and the degree of complicity in the sin. This incongruity has become the basis of seemingly endless debates regarding atonement in the Christian West.[1]

When Christians hold and pass down interpretations of Scripture, they gradually become taken for granted as unequivocal expressions of "what the Bible says." While there is nothing necessarily wrong with traditional modes of interpretation, they become problematic when they harbor subtle fallacies that render the Scriptures themselves questionable, not just the interpretive lens being

---

1   The debate specifically takes the form of the relocation of punishment for sin from a person to another living creature. In the case of the Old Testament, this is generally a sacrificial animal. It should be noted that nowhere in the text of the Old Testament are sins applied to a sacrificial animal, nor are sacrificial animals ever made to suffer, nor is the killing of the animal ever ritualized as a punishment. The sole instance of applying sins to an animal is the scapegoat within the Day of Atonement ritual. The scapegoat is not, and cannot be, sacrificed once it is bearing the sins of the people. All these misinterpretations of the Old Testament are then typically applied to Christ's death in the New Testament.

applied. There will always be passages in the Scriptures that seem difficult to square with human rationality. Most often, the difficulty stems from our own understanding (or lack thereof), not with the text. The issue of sin is one such example—the problem is not the Scriptures or how they speak of sin, but rather the way we have come to read the Scriptures.

To better grasp how the Scriptures conceive of and deal with sin, we must become familiar with how its authors saw sin.

The Physical Taint of Sin

FROM THE BEGINNING, THE BOOK of Genesis depicts sin as having a corrupting influence, not only on humanity but on the physical created order. In Genesis 3, neither Adam nor Eve is cursed; rather, the curse falls on the serpent (3:14) and the ground, which is cursed because of Adam's disobedience (3:17). The ground's curse would cause perpetual challenges for humanity from this point, in the form of aridity—a lack of cooperation with humanity to cultivate and sustain life from the soil. Thus, human rebellion is directly responsible for the pollution of the earth.

This is not the only time humanity's sinfulness has a detrimental impact on the created order, which is an ongoing theme in the Torah. Abel's innocent blood taints the earth and cries out from it, as does the blood of other murdered innocents (Gen. 4:10; Deut. 21:1–9). While the corruption of sin originated in Cain's act, it continues and escalates through the early chapters of Genesis. At Noah's birth, his father, Lamech, describes the purpose of the Flood prophetically as freeing the earth and humanity from the curse brought upon it by human sin (Gen. 5:29). Deuteronomy 28:20–24 elaborates on the curses of the Torah in full, dividing them into two categories: those by which the created order is tainted by human sin, and those by which God purges sinful humanity from the land to correct that taint.

The First Epistle of John locates the origin of human sin and corruption not in Adam and his disobedience in the garden, but rather in Cain and his act of fratricide (3:11–18). This emphasis is not unique to 1 John but is a typical feature of Second Temple literature. Jewish works of scriptural interpretation, at least those still in existence, commonly point to Cain as the source of sin's corruption, indicating this was a majority view by the first century AD. Early Christian interpretations of Genesis retained this understanding.

Though Genesis presents Adam's choice to eat from the tree of knowledge as the first trespass of divine command that brings about death and curses, Genesis does not describe Adam's action with the word *sin*. This term is not used until Genesis 4:7, which describes sin as a crouching animal or a malicious power seeking to master Cain, not as a transgression of a commandment per se. Cain is also the first agent of human death in the murder of his brother. Though his parents were mortal, neither had died at the time of Abel's murder, making Abel the first human to fall victim to death. These distinctions led to a vast swathe of early Jewish and Christian interpreters understanding Cain as the primary human agent of sin and death in the world.

Wisdom of Solomon's tenth chapter gives an extensive listing of the enemies of wisdom who, therefore, become enemies of the righteous. Cain is the first listed and is the only person this list describes as "unrighteous" (10:3). Beyond merely the first sinner and the offender in the first murder, an act of fratricide, Cain is the archetype of all sin and wickedness. Wisdom goes on, however, to ascribe to Cain responsibility for the Flood many generations later (10:4). Not only does Cain bear guilt and responsibility for his crimes, but his crimes pollute the world in a way that ultimately brings destruction upon the whole created order.

Josephus, a Pharisee and Jewish historian of the first century, likewise posits Cain as the originator and archetypal figure related to human sin.[2] He describes Cain not only as unrighteous but as "most evil," not only an unrepentant doer of evil but also a teacher of evil who actively promoted evil to his descendants. Therefore, each generation of Cain's descendants became even more wicked than the generation before. Cain set in motion a cycle of corruption and pollution of the world, which ultimately led to the Flood as a divine means of purifying the corrupted created order.[3] He does this not passively by being the first in a series of sinners but actively by sinning and teaching wickedness. Josephus thus sees Cain as the founder and originator of sin and its corrupting effects on the world.

It is in this context that early Christian interpreters understood the genealogy of Cain (Gen. 4:17–22) as a continued snowballing of sin and wickedness through each subsequent generation. In this passage, the figure of Lamech is of greatest consequence as the only figure described in any detail. In addition to being the end of Cain's genealogy as recorded in Genesis, Lamech is seven generations after Adam. Seven is a number used throughout the Old Testament to convey fullness or completion.[4] Lamech's position in Cain's genealogy, the seventh, parallels Enoch in that of Seth (Gen. 5:21–24). Perhaps most relevant to this discussion, however, is that the genealogy cites Lamech as the first to practice polygamy (Gen. 4:19). In the minds of early interpreters, this ties him not merely to the abhorrent bloodshed of Cain (after whom he names one of his sons), but also to sexual sin.

---

2   In addition to providing an important perspective on many events of the New Testament era, Josephus serves as a repository for Jewish traditions as they stood in the first century. Josephus describes these Cain traditions in *Antiquities* 1.53–66.

3   This idea of Cain as an active teacher of wickedness caused him to be identified as the first heretic. Jude 11 makes this connection in the New Testament. Outside of the Scriptures, Philo of Alexandria, the Aramaic Targums, Clement of Alexandria, and Tertullian also identify Cain as a heretic.

4   Saint Augustine sees Lamech as the fulfillment of the line of Cain. *City of God*, 15.17.

Commenting on this passage, Josephus views Cain's sin as motivated by the need to quench bodily desire. Lamech's sins are the same as his ancestor's but multiplied exponentially. The sons of Lamech, with their described occupations, represent various divisions of the sin and wickedness Cain brought into the world. Both Philo[5] and Josephus see Cain's propensity for metallurgy as symbolic of an orientation toward war and mass murder, making it a kind of culmination of Cain's original sin of murder.[6] It is the consistent interpretation of the Aramaic Targums at Genesis 4:26 that the sons of Lamech were also associated with the origin of idolatry and thereby sexual immorality. In these sources, the sexual immorality of Genesis 6:1–4 is a sin attributed to Cain's female descendants, who seduced the angelic beings.

Just as Cain's evil is magnified in future generations of his descendants, so also is his curse. Early interpreters see the curse of Cain in terms of his relationship to the created order. God cursed the ground because of Adam's disobedience, making it burdensome for him to work the land (Gen. 3:17). Cain, by contrast, was cursed "from the ground" (4:11). Early interpreters understood the reverse phrasing to indicate Cain's sin was more serious than Adam's. Others perceived a continuity between the two—for Pseudo-Philo, an element of Cain's curse fell upon the earth itself, furthering the corruption set in motion by Adam's disobedience.

The deepening of the curse because of the growth of Cain's wickedness turned the alienation of Adam from the earth, which produced hardship in agricultural endeavors, to a state of outright hostility by the created order. The curse made it impossible for Cain

---

5   Philo of Alexandria was a first-century Jewish author living in Egypt. His writings combine insights from Jewish tradition and Greek learning. He is generally considered part of the philosophical movement called "Middle Platonism."

6   Philo, *Posterity*, 116–117.

to continue an agricultural way of life (Gen. 4:2), prompting him to build a city, thereby establishing his descendants' ties to urban life (4:17–22). Philo understands the earth's enmity toward Cain to encompass all the elements—bodies of freshwater as well as the sun, moon, and stars of heaven.[7] Finally, the corruption of his sin incites hostility in wild animals, according to Philo and Josephus.

The central theme of the Torah is maintaining ritual and moral purity within the camp—and later the nation—of Israel. The opposite of purity, in Greek, is *agos*, "accursed," understood as a state of ritual impurity caused by certain sacrilegious crimes, including the murder of an innocent victim or a family member. It was impossible to atone for this form of ritual impurity. Cain is the "accursed" one par excellence for Philo, who uses that term to describe Cain five times.[8] Four of these examples also include the word for fratricide (*adelphoktonos*, literally "brother-slayer"), implying this was the reason for Cain's impurity/accursedness.

In the context of ancient understandings of Genesis, then, Cain functions as the archetypal sinner. His trespass, and the curse by which it contaminates the created order, is likewise a microcosm of the effects of all human sin on the world. The most serious sins— namely idolatry, sexual immorality, and murder—tainted the earth itself and demanded sinful humanity be expunged for it to be purified (Lev. 18:24–28). Sin and wickedness, far from violations of arbitrarily imposed "rules," are evil because they destroy right relationship between humanity and the created order. Sin disrupts justice and leaves a potentially permanent mark not only on the soul but also on the body and on the physical, material order. It cannot, therefore, merely be overlooked but must be dealt with.

---

7   Philo, *Questions and Solutions in Genesis*, 1.71–74.
8   Philo, *Worse*, 96; *Posterity*, 49; *Husbandry*, 21; *Virtues*, 199; *Questions and Answers in Genesis*, 1.77.

Quarantine

IN THE TORAH, THE RELATIONSHIP between sin and the order built into creation first emerges in Genesis 3:17, when the ground became cursed because of Adam's sin. While some would interpret this curse as a fractured relationship merely between Adam and the rest of the creation, the theme of the land itself becoming tainted is carried through the Holiness Code of Leviticus, in which particular sins—among them sexual immorality—are said to defile the land itself (18:24). For God to return to dwell in the land, it must first be purified, and this purification will destroy sinful humanity if the people do not first purify themselves and the sanctuary. Why the sanctuary? Because the defilement of the people also caused the sanctuary to become defiled, regardless of whether their sinful acts actually occurred there. The sanctuary, after all, is where God dwells with His people, and their state of being has effects for this sacred space.

As an example, Leviticus 20:3 states that anyone from the people of Israel who offers a child to Molech is to be cut off because they have defiled the sanctuary. It is not reasonable to surmise that this penalty was due to those who constructed a shrine to Molech only within the courts of the tabernacle or the later temple. Rather, such an act, committed anywhere by one of God's people, defiles the sanctuary and the name of God Himself.

While idolatry involving human sacrifice is a serious sin, the sanctuary could be defiled even from ritual impurity that was not sinful. The Torah distinguishes between sin and uncleanness—sin was dealt with primarily through sacrifice, uncleanness through ceremonial washings. In Numbers 19:13, those who have touched a corpse defile not only themselves but also the tabernacle if they do not perform the proper cleansing ritual. If they do not perform ritual washings, their defilement remains upon them, in which case the defilement extends to the tabernacle, even for individuals who did not enter the tabernacle or its courts. While the distinction here between ritual impurity and sin as such is real, the refusal to follow the prescribed cleansing ritual is itself an act of disobedience, thereby adding sin to uncleanness.

This dynamic of uncleansed impurity extending defilement to the sanctuary represents a major source of the contamination, which requires cleansing through the Day of Atonement ritual from the sanctuary. What is true of uncleanness that is ignored is also true of sin when the person who committed it does not repent or make the relevant purification offerings. God's presence among His people demands holiness from people and sanctuary. Although the Torah allowed for the restoration of that holiness after becoming impure or defiled, this required the person responsible to cooperate by undergoing the appropriate ritual. To refuse would endanger the whole people, which is why the Day of Atonement called for the high priest to cleanse this impurity on behalf of the community, even without the cooperation or participation of everyone who dwelled there. The cleansing of impurity from the sanctuary and camp left the unpurified or unconfessed to suffer the consequences of rebellion alone. The ritual of the Day of Atonement removed the curse or stain left by the sin and impurity of community members from the sanctuary and community, but not from persons who refused to participate.

The communal and sacramental implications of individual sins meant that any act committed by anyone in the community was a potential source of contamination. This reality heightens the warning found in Leviticus 15:31 that the pollution of the tabernacle through impurity contracted by the people of Israel would result in their death. The warning refers not only to those who approach the tabernacle to make an offering while in a state of uncleanness or sin, but also to those who have defiled the sanctuary from a distance. The threat is that the people involved in the defilement of the tabernacle will die instead of being exiled so that God will not have to depart from their midst. The Day of Atonement ritual, performed correctly by the high priest, prevented God from removing Himself from Israel.

The concrete nature of sin and defilement here does not mean that they are physical phenomena occupying time and space. This is ritual language—the entities it describes (not only sin or defilement but also God and other spiritual beings) are indeed real, but not in a physical or material sense. It would be misguided to try to determine how sin or corruption "travels" to the sanctuary from the place where an act is committed or from the person who commits the act. Every Israelite is connected to God by being part of His people and so is in His presence, even when not in the physical location that God has chosen in which to meet with His people. God's presence is not restricted to His sanctuary, and therefore the defilement of that sanctuary is possible at any point where He is present.

The ambivalence of the Torah regarding the special holiness of the tabernacle and later temple and priesthood, on the one hand, and the calling of the entire nation to be a holy nation and a kingdom of priests on the other (Ex. 19:6) reflects this understanding. The priesthood was set apart as individuals and families from the rest of Israel as holy. Yet all the people of Israel were called not only to consecrate themselves at the ratification of the covenant initially but also to maintain holiness through the ritual means prescribed by the Torah. Likewise, the tabernacle and later the temple, as a sanctuary, were set apart as holy to be the place where the Lord dwelt, yet the whole camp and then the nation was called to be set apart from all the other nations of the world as holy to the Lord their God. There is, therefore, no zone in which an Israelite is allowed to become and remain defiled or to commit sin without consequence. Exile from God's presence, as in the case of the scapegoat on the Day of Atonement, brings about destruction, not freedom.

While not directly related to the sanctuary as such, the Torah contains additional examples of ritual impurity and sin affecting the material world through means other than direct contact. In Numbers 19:14–15, any open vessels that were in a space occupied by a corpse, whether or not they touched the body directly, are unclean until purified. Likewise, the remains of the sacrificed animals used in the Day of Atonement ritual were still treated and disposed of as things defiled, even though their deaths were for sacrificial offerings and their blood was used to purify the sanctuary. In Numbers 19, participants in the burning of the red heifer are defiled, although its ashes are not considered unclean while it is burning. In Leviticus 14:34–36, the contents of a leper's house are considered unclean, but only after a priest has pronounced the house to be contaminated with the sickness. Objects taken from the home before this official determination remain clean. The contamination is therefore based not on physical contact or even proximity but instead on ritual determination and concern.

These considerations share in common an underlying view of sin as a contaminant, at least at a ritual level. This idea challenges an understanding of sin as the transgression of a commandment or similar views that hold sin to be a primarily legal category. Sin in the Torah is not only a deadly disease but a contagious one that, unless it or the perpetrator is cut off from the people, will infect not only the sanctuary but the entire community. These two understandings of sin, the legal and the epidemiological, are not mutually exclusive. The violation of the laws and commandments of God, though requiring legal punishment, are remedied by rituals of purification and cleansing. The clearest example is the Day of Atonement ritual proper and the scapegoat in particular. The high priest confesses the sins of the people, a confession that seeks mercy in the face of justice over the goat. The goat then bears the sins of the people away. The sins carried by the goat "infect" the one who leads the goat from the camp, making him ceremonially unclean.

Blood Atonement

AS ALREADY MENTIONED, THE PRIMARY way the curse and corruption created by human sin were resolved within the sanctuary was through the Day of Atonement ritual described in Leviticus 16. Ritual, as delineated in the Torah, contains a strong element of reenactment, not simply for the sake of remembrance, but also to allow the participants to experience the event being reenacted and share its effects. One clear example of this occurs in the rituals surrounding the Passover, the first of the major commemorations the Torah commands Israel to observe. Only unleavened bread is to be used in the meal, as though preparing hastily for a journey. Those who take part in this ritual also participate in the event and thereby experience God delivering them from bondage (Ex. 12:11; 13:8). This same paradigm plays out in ritual sacrifice and the rituals prescribed for the Day of Atonement. The liturgics of sacrifice reenact the breaking of covenant relationship with God through death, followed by ritually enacting the restoration of that relationship.

The Day of Atonement ritual is introduced not as an acontextual set of liturgical commands but as a response to the deaths of Nadab and Abihu, the sons of Aaron. These two had entered the tabernacle and offered incense to God in an inappropriate manner, then were struck dead. The first stages of the ritual, in particular, are the procedures for the high priest to safely enter into the presence of God using incense and a personal sin offering. God's presence itself is purgative, and to survive that presence, the high priest must have already cleansed himself of sin and defilement. He ritually enacts this cleansing through both the act of sacrifice and the covering cloud of incense, which prevents him from directly beholding the presence of God face to face.

The consuming fire of His holiness means that the presence of God in the midst of the people represents a danger to them. The danger is not the result of some ill intent or inherently wrathful nature of God but rather because sin and anything unclean cannot exist in His presence. The initial purification and consecration of the tabernacle and its furnishings, as well as the consecration of the priests and the people, produced a status quo within which God could safely dwell among them in the tabernacle. By defiling the sanctuary, sin and uncleanness in the camp disrupted this equilibrium. Even the stain left by these acts made God's presence in the camp no longer safe for priests or people, which is why ritual atonement must take place to reestablish this status quo. Not only must the priests and people be reconsecrated, but the tabernacle and all its utensils and furnishings must also be rededicated.

A given ceremonial act can have multiple meanings in varying contexts. For example, while the Day of Atonement ritual includes two sin offerings that are similar to those performed to forgive sins in individual cases, their presence within the remainder of the ritual gives them a new context that provides them with an additional and somewhat different meaning. The ritual act itself is distinct from the meaning ascribed to it.

The meaning of these actions is not merely an abstract, theological concept. Rather, the meaning of a ritual is its goal—that which the proper performance of the ritual accomplishes. A ritual does something or is at least seen to do something, and this purpose forms its meaning. So, for example, the meaning of the sprinkling of blood in the sanctuary can be said to be the purging of impurity and sin, because this is what the proper performance of the sprinkling as a ritual accomplishes.

The ritual immediately entails the death of two animals, though the text does not describe their death in any great detail as to mode, manner, or place. The key focus in Leviticus 16 is rather on what is to be done with the blood. The death of the animals, therefore, is a means to an end in extracting their blood, which the following chapter will further explain by identifying the blood as the life of the animal. Their killing does not involve cruelty or the infliction of pain for any ritual purpose. These animals were killed quickly and cleanly in order to extract their blood. The blood is then taken and repurposed. Additionally, the sacrificial act is seen to be a repetition of the action that broke the status quo, or an enactment of the potential threat that the act seeks to alleviate. The animals, however, are slaughtered only after first having been presented before God, and this in and of itself is part of the ritual offering as a "setting forth," in Greek, *anaphora*.[9]

In another episode of sacrificial mimicry, the two goats suffer the two fates threatened for disobedience to the prescriptions of the Torah, namely death and exile, both of which represent destruction. The scapegoat, which carried the sins of the people outside of the camp, is called the "goat for Azazel" (Azazel was understood to be a demonic force existing in the desert). Nevertheless, the one who leads the scapegoat out of the camp does not actively kill it, ritually or otherwise; rather, it is left to its fate in the harsh wilderness outside the camp. Being abandoned by God to the world—with its oppressive authorities from whom God had delivered the people from Egypt and represented here by the figure of Azazel—typifies a fate that is darker than physical death. These rituals communicate to Israel the two possible outcomes of God's presence mixing with an unclean and sinful people: either the fire of His presence will consume the people, or God will depart from them.

The central ritual act connected to the purification of physical space and its contents is the use of the blood extracted from the bull

---

9   This sacrificial term is used for the central portion of the Orthodox Divine Liturgy in which the Eucharist is consecrated.

and the sacrificial goat. The blood is drained from the animals and collected. The high priest then takes it into the holiest place and sprinkles it, after offering the protective cloud of incense. The sanctuary sanctifies the blood as sacrificial. It is then able to be used to sanctify and cleanse the altar. The high priest sprinkles and spreads the blood throughout the sanctuary, physically and symbolically covering everything. As they lead to death, sin and rebellion are represented by the destruction of life by killing and the shedding of blood. The sacred, sacrificial blood is spread and covers the blood of innocent victims, which cries out for vengeance, with blood that is holy and pure (Gen. 4:10). This idea of blood covering blood is brought out plainly in Numbers 35:33, in which only the blood of the murderer can cover over the blood of the murder victim as it cries out from the land that has been polluted. In the New Testament, this dynamic is made explicit in describing the atoning function of Christ's shed blood (Heb. 12:24).

Blood is used in the ritual in this way, as a purifying agent regarding the material sanctuary, in only two cases. Blood was used to purify the outer altar as a means of consecrating it for the offering. The other case is the ritual of the Day of Atonement itself, in which it was used on the altar as well as within the innermost holy place. Blood in this context of purification offerings is applied only to the physical objects of the tabernacle, especially the altar, and not to human persons. There are, however, other offerings in which blood is sprinkled upon the people, notably in the covenant affirmation at Sinai (Ex. 24:5–8), for the ordination of priests (Lev. 8:22–24), and at the healing of certain skin diseases (Lev. 14:12–14, 25). In these cases, the blood is also sprinkled on an altar, creating a blood-based connection between God and the people who have been sprinkled.

Although the blood sprinkled on the altar ritually purifies the altar and the other elements of the sanctuary, in the remainder of the Levitical legislation, the blood that covers the sin or uncleanness that taints the sanctuary absorbs the contamination and therefore is treated as a defiled and dangerous substance. In Leviticus 6:20, for instance, if blood that has been used for holy purposes splashes on a garment, the garment becomes unclean—not purified—by that contact. It must be purified through ritual washing, and the pot in which it was cleansed must be destroyed.

This defilement of the garment explains why the high priest did not sprinkle the sacrificial blood on the people on the Day of Atonement. The blood used on the Day of Atonement worked forgiveness of the people by purifying the sanctuary, not by covering their sins (in which case the blood would be sprinkled or wiped on them). The purification of the sins of the individual offerers is handled through the repetitive sin and guilt offerings throughout the year and is applied to them ritually in those contexts. By the time the annual Day of Atonement arrived, persons who had contracted ritual impurity or who had sinned had either made use of the provided remedies through cleansing and offerings or had suffered the punishments, notably death or exile, for their refusal to do so. The Day of Atonement itself, then, purged sins not from the people but from the sanctuary.

The cleansing of the sanctuary with blood is rightly called an atonement "for the sanctuary," although the sanctuary is not capable of sinning. It purges away and removes the defilement, which accumulates as an obstacle, obstructing the relationship between God and His people. This obstruction must be dealt with, and the ritual metaphors of wiping away, purging, cleansing, or covering over all deal with the removal of such an obstruction.

The language of atonement is used in this way in nonliturgical contexts as well. A prime example occurs in Genesis 32:21. Before meeting his brother, Esau, Jacob seeks to atone for his past wrongs, literally to "cover Esau's face," hoping to reconcile. To make reconciliation possible, he removes the matter of contention by giving offerings to his brother. He cannot reconcile his brother to himself simply by desiring it. He can, however, facilitate and make possible such a reconciliation.

Likewise, when the language of atonement concerns God in the context of rituals like the Day of Atonement, God is neither the subject nor the object of the verb. A ritual does not reconcile God to the offerer like a magic trick. Neither does God atone people to Himself. Instead, the defilement—in particular of the sanctuary—has come between God and His people and must be cleansed to restore the relationship and communion reflected by the presence of the tabernacle in the midst of the camp.

The verb "forgive" does not appear in Leviticus 16, nor in either of the other passages that deal with the prescribed rituals for the Day of Atonement (Lev. 23:26–32; Num. 29:7–11). Emphasis on forgiveness, as well as on fasting and other ascetic practices for Yom Kippur, came later, in the Rabbinic period. Although purification and cleansing do enact forgiveness, that is not the ultimate aim. Rather, these rites seek to remove sin and defilement and thus restore the order within the camp, with God dwelling at its center, that had prevailed after the liberation of the people of Israel from Egypt. The removal of sin and corruption represents a return to freedom from its harmful effects—freedom to serve Israel's God.

There are, in fact, not-so-subtle shades of the Passover ritual contained within the Day of Atonement ritual. The fate of the goat driven into the wilderness to Azazel is essentially parallel to the fate of the Israelites under the oppression of the Egyptians and their gods, against whom God rendered judgment in the Passover event (Ex. 12:12). Likewise, the smearing of blood here reconstitutes the people of God, who were first constituted through the smearing of blood on doorposts in Egypt (v. 13). Israel was freed from serving Pharaoh to serve God. Atonement does away with the sin and defilement resulting from Israel's disobedience, which impedes that service, allowing this service to begin anew. Through the Day of Atonement's ritual enactment, Israel is restored to its newborn state.

While caution is important when utilizing cross-cultural comparisons, Babylonian and Ugaritic rituals also enact the purging of the temple from the forces of defeated evil. However, sin and uncleanness in the temple of the Israelites is not personified as evil spirits. Instead, sin is represented as a malignant force that attaches itself to the physical tabernacle and its contents.

Rather than defeating these forces in battle, the priests purge the sin and defilement, seen as an ontological reality, from the tabernacle and its furnishings. The tabernacle is then once again holy and able to accommodate God's presence. The holiness of this space keeps the malign spiritual powers represented by Azazel at the margins of the community—either the borders of the camp in the wilderness or the later national border. The ability of the high priest to place the sins of the people onto the scapegoat, and the goat's capacity to carry those sins away into the wilderness, both also imply the substantial reality of sin.

Leviticus, indeed the entire Torah, envision sin and uncleanness not merely as legal infractions or ceremonial status, respectively, but as ontological realities among the people, in particular within the tabernacle, the center of their life. God's holiness purifies the area of His presence in a way that threatens either to destroy the people with their sins or to force them out of His presence and back into the world from which He had redeemed them.

When the Scriptures speak of Christ's atoning sacrifice, as in Hebrews and 1 John, His self-offering on the Cross is seen in these same terms of the removal of sin and purification from its stain by sacred blood, though with Christ as ultimate fulfillment. Christ bears the sins of the people, taking them outside of the city and removing them (Heb. 13:12). Christ's blood purifies not only an earthly sanctuary in the midst of the world but the whole world (1 John 2:2).

The sacrificial system of the Old Testament is not the slaughter of innocent creatures in order to appease the wrath of an angry god with their blood. It is the means of the purification of sin, which allows human persons to draw close to God once again and share a sacred meal of communion. The death of sacrificial victims was not ritualized and, therefore, not part of the meaning of sacrifice. While very detailed instructions are given for other elements of sacrificial rituals, none are given for the means of killing the animals involved. To sacrifice something is not to kill it, but to eat it as a sacred meal. This required its death, whether the sacrifice was of animals or plants (such as firstfruits from the harvest and grain offerings). Sins were not placed upon sacrificed animals, and they were in no wise punished or caused to suffer. Likewise, the death of Christ is not the ultimate example of God avenging His justice through punishing His Son. Rather, it is the Son offering Himself up to be eaten as food by the faithful to purify them of sin and to share with them His eternal, divine life.

CHAPTER

4

Spiritual
Warfare

ORIGEN FAMOUSLY SAID THAT THE narratives of Joshua would be immoral if they did not have the character (*figura*) of spiritual warfare. This statement has often been misinterpreted as championing what is now called an allegorical interpretation of the Scriptures. This reduces Origen's comment—not to mention his subsequent commentary on the Book of Joshua—to effectively mean "what this book contains is horrible, so we must read it all figuratively." Yet this is not the methodology Origen employed throughout the rest of the commentary on Joshua. It is not as though he considered the book abhorrent, salvageable only by putting a certain allegorical or moral "spin" on it. Rather, for him, even if a surface reading of the text may prove challenging or problematic at certain points, the Book of Joshua is *really* about spiritual warfare. It is talking about spiritual warfare when interpreted correctly.

The theme of spiritual warfare does not begin in Joshua but rather in the Torah, with its account of the Exodus and the early battles precipitated by Israel's arrival at the lands east of the Jordan River. This continuity is so striking that it has led some scholars to speak of a

Hexateuch, to include Joshua. Nor does Joshua conclude the discussion of spiritual warfare, which continues into the Books of Samuel/Kingdoms. One could even argue that the theme of spiritual warfare does not fully resolve until the Revelation of St. John at the end of the New Testament. The New Testament depiction of spiritual warfare is related to that of Joshua not merely allegorically or analogically, but quite directly and literally.

The Book of Joshua, therefore, is not exceptional in its treatment of these themes. It cannot be singled out or ignored as a uniquely problematic text, since it is fully integrated with and characteristic of the rest of Scripture. Based on precisely the type of surface reading of which Origen warned, however, it has become the intense focus of arguments that see biblical, and especially Old Testament, violence as problematic. In describing the narrative of the book, modern commentators—scholars and laypeople alike—commonly assert that in Joshua, God orders the genocide of various ethnic groups of Canaanites. This is treated as self-evident—God unequivocally commanded the indiscriminate killing of women and children. In this matrix, anyone seeking to defend or even understand how the Book of Joshua portrays the Israelite conquest of the land of Canaan is effectively condoning genocide. After all, if someone willingly rationalizes violence, warfare, and the displacement of people in the Scriptures, what's to stop them from justifying such evil at other points in history, including in the present?

It is grievous that throughout history, the Scriptures—by manipulative or simply weak interpretations—have been marshalled to justify sin and even mass atrocities. While slavery may be the most obvious example, one need look no further than the American myth of "Manifest Destiny"[1] to find a vile application of Joshua in particu-

---

1   Manifest Destiny was the belief, common in the nineteenth century, that God had given the greater part of the North American continent to American colonizers. This belief not only justified but demanded the killing and

lar. Yet it is likewise true that genocides and conquests have occurred in history without any reference to the Scriptures. Such wicked deeds were justified by their perpetrators, instead, with some recourse to a philosophy, religious teaching, political ideal, or even an appeal to some scientific theory. Yet although the Scriptures are not the only basis used to justify evil, they have become a kind of weapon of choice in a culture as steeped in Christianity as the West is, or at least has been.

All the Gods of the Nations Are Demons

PSALM 96/95:5 BLUNTLY STATES, "ALL the gods of the nations are demons." Saint Paul reaffirms this when he says, "What the nations sacrifice, they sacrifice to demons" (1 Cor. 10:20). The common presupposition in the modern West is that the ancient gods worshipped by the nations surrounding Israel are not real. We assume they are figments of a superstitious cultural imagination—primitive attempts at explaining material, natural phenomena in a prescientific way. Religious disagreements between ancient tribes and nations, at best, are seen as just one more element of tribal identity, along with language and other markers. At worst, the religious beliefs of ancient peoples are considered pure superstition. They have no positive value and merely served to impel their followers toward irrational and ultimately destructive actions.

Reading the Scriptures from this perspective leads to distorted interpretations. All invective, denunciations, and threats of judgment are presumed to be directed by one group of humans against another group of humans, since (at least from our modern vantage point) no other personal beings exist. Similarly, violence between

displacement of native populations to make way for American expansion in fulfilling a divinely given destiny.

groups is motivated only by prejudices, desires, and material interests. While this worldview may be a relevant lens for assessing modern historical events, it was simply not the way participants in biblical events and history perceived their world. More importantly, the authors of the texts that comprise Scripture did not hold these presuppositions and thus had no intention of conveying them through the events they recorded.

Ironically, the critics most determined to force a material, historical reading onto biblical texts in order to condemn them simultaneously deny that these events actually took place. Although they hold the death of the firstborn males of Egypt to be unconscionable, they simultaneously believe it was entirely fictional. They likewise point to the conquest under Joshua as being a record of genocide but again deny that any such conquest ever happened. In some cases, they argue for events not actually described in the text but, as they say, hidden by it, and proceed to condemn the Scriptures for their reconstructed events. One prominent example of this is the belief, commonplace for decades among scholars, that consecrating the firstborn sons of Israel to Yahweh (Ex. 13:1–2) was "really" a guise for child sacrifice. Religions that hold these texts to be sacred are then condemned for the hypothetical, horrible acts that they supposedly conceal.

In order to properly assess a text and its teaching, it must be read in context. This context includes not only the date and place of its writing and the ancient language in which it is written, but also the understanding and worldview of its author(s). Regardless of a given reader's beliefs, the authors of Scripture believed that God, angels, demons, the spirits of the dead, and other spiritual realities were real. They held them to be as real as rocks, trees, and humans. It is in light of those beliefs that they formulate their writings and interpret events, words, and actions. When readers refuse to enter into the worldview of an author, they end up constructing a false "reality" as a backdrop for the text. They then praise or attack that reality, even if it is false, misguided, anachronistic, or pure fiction. Condemning such fictional reconstructions should not be confused with a legitimate critique of the text itself.

For all ancient peoples, the gods of neighboring nations were not fictional. From the perspective of the authors of the Hebrew Scriptures, the spiritual beings worshipped by other tribes, clans, and nations surrounding them were real. Frequently in the Old Testament, the word *gods* is even used to describe them. They were not God in the sense that Yahweh is God, but rather spirits created by Yahweh, their God, along with everything else that exists, and who had since their creation fallen into rebellion against Him. These were spirits that sought the destruction of humanity.

Ancient Israel understood these "gods" of the nations to have been assigned to those nations by Yahweh, the Most High God, at one particular point. As part of the judgment against humanity at the Tower of Babel, described in Genesis 11, God distanced Himself from the nations of the world, assigning angelic beings to shepherd them (Deut. 32:8). The nations were not to worship these beings, nor were these beings to seek to be worshipped (Deut. 4:19). They were not only to shepherd the nations in the sense of governance but to religiously shepherd them back to the Most High God. Other than St. Michael, who was assigned to the nation of Israel, these beings failed in this assignment.[2]

Yahweh, the God of Israel, has promised to judge all of creation and restore it to justice, its rightful order. This justification of the cosmos includes not only the visible, material world and human persons but also the invisible world of angels and demons. Several points in Scripture make this judgment explicit. Isaiah, for example, states, "In that day, Yahweh will punish the host of heaven above and the kings

---

2   Saint Dionysios the Areopagite describes this in some detail in *The Celestial Hierarchy*.

of the earth below" (24:21). The culmination of this final judgment is not only a new earth but also a new heaven (Rev. 21:1). The lake of fire as a description of eternal condemnation was created not for humans but for the devil and his angels (Matt. 25:41). This particular judgment, the judgment of the powers and principalities both in the heavenly places and on the earth, is known as the death of the gods because of its description in Psalm 82/81.

Just as is the case with humanity, the judgment of these principalities and powers, spiritual kings and rulers of nations, is not entirely put off to the end but intrudes at various points in history. The ten plagues that trigger nascent Israel's Exodus from Egypt are described as Yahweh rendering judgment against the gods of Egypt (Ex. 12:12). It should go without saying that from the perspective of the author of Exodus, God is not judging or punishing a group of fictional characters. The gods of Egypt are seen as real spiritual beings who have led the Egyptian people into wickedness and evil. These principalities are the ones whom Yahweh, the God of Israel, holds most responsible for the evils of the Egyptian Empire and culture.

The humans who populated Egypt were moral agents responsible for their actions. They suffered the consequences when judgment came upon Egypt, and God leveled the scales, restoring justice. By directing the plagues of Egypt against the gods of Egypt, however, Yahweh not only judges those spirits but also conveys truth to the Egyptian people. The primary task of the pharoah, in the Egyptian understanding, was to establish and maintain *ma'at*, justice. As king and priest, it was his task to make sure that relations between gods, humans, the river, and the land were maintained for continued prosperity. His inability to restore justice exposed him and the other Egyptian gods to be frauds, along with the illusion of their power, might, and worthiness to be worshiped.

Though the Israelites were enslaved, literally, to Pharaoh and the Egyptian nobility, the common people of Egypt were no less enslaved in a spiritual sense. Yahweh not only redeemed Israel from Egypt; He also offered the truth of who He is to the Egyptians themselves, which had the potential to set them free. The condemnation in the Hebrew Scriptures of the gods and god-kings of the nations is not a condemnation of the humans who make up those tribes and clans. It is instead a condemnation of those who have oppressed, abused, and enslaved those people. An interpretation that delineates between the spiritual/political powers oppressing a nation and the people *of* that nation does not allegorize the text away or deny its historicity. It is simply a lens that validates the distinction that the authors of these texts establish and see as important. In other words, it is an example of reading biblical texts correctly and in context.

The Christian Old Testament is filled with texts calling for judgment and condemnation, and even the deaths, of kings and rulers and principalities over the nations. Psalm 149/148 speaks of the saints carrying two-edged swords in their hands "to execute vengeance on the nations and judgments on the tribes by binding their kings with chains and their nobles with iron chains, in order to execute on them the judgment of the Scriptures" (vv. 7–9). Isaiah speaks of the demonic powers of Sheol being punished and never rising again (26:14). In the Greek text, the translator adds the interjection, "Bring more evils upon them, O Lord, bring more evils upon them who are glorious upon the earth" (vv. 14–15). The "them" of this call for justice is quite clearly these aforementioned demonic powers of Hades.

Examples abound, but one passage in particular is of note for its prominence in discussions of imprecations within the Christian Old Testament. Psalm 137/136 is a psalm written in Babylonian exile. This exile in a foreign, pagan empire is the theme of the psalm itself, beginning with the question as to whether it is even possible to truly worship Yahweh in a foreign land (v. 4). The worship of Judah's God was so closely associated with Zion, with the Jerusalem temple, that attempting to offer such worship, even only through hymns, seemed difficult in light of its destruction (vv. 1–3). The memory of Jerusalem was key to the continuation of that worship (vv. 5–6). This is not merely nostalgia for a time and place now lost, but the memory of all that transpired in Judah's wickedness and the subsequent judgment.

The psalm then takes what many modern readers understand to be a sharp turn. It speaks of the nation of Edom and its actions at the fall of Jerusalem to Babylon (Ps. 137/136:7). It speaks of Edom as a daughter of Babylon, a loyal collaborator of Judah's oppressor (v. 8). It states that the one who takes vengeance against Edom will be blessed, in particular the one who smashes Edom's little ones against the rocks (v. 9). A literal reading of this psalm, the reading that has made it controversial, understands this to be an angry and bitter human in exile calling for the violent murder of Edomite babies as retribution.

The subtext here, however, is the long history between Edom and Judah, which includes an overarching spiritual dimension. Judah and Edom are descended from Jacob and Esau, Israel and Edom, respectively. These two brothers experienced conflict and ultimate reconciliation, as described in Genesis. Edom had received a portion of Abraham's inheritance as his descendants, but this involved a vassal relationship with Israel and later Judah. Some of the Edomites, as described in the psalm and in the historical accounts of Jerusalem's fall, took pleasure and rejoiced in that fall, seeing it as freedom despite their now being vassals of Babylon.

The author of Psalm 137/136 and other ancient Judahites understood there to be a spiritual cause behind Edom's schadenfreude over Judah's fate. Just as St. Michael the archangel was seen to be the guardian angel of Israel and later Judah as a nation (Dan. 12:1), Edom was guarded and governed by the fallen archangel Samael, who is often equated with Satan in Jewish writings of the period during and following the exile. Only such an evil spirit could have inspired Edom's rejoicing in Judah's devastation. The psalmist seeks the destruction of this demonic spirit at the hand of Yahweh, the Blessed One.

This understanding of this psalm led the Church Fathers, nearly uniformly, to understand the "little ones" here spoken of not as infant humans of Edomite ethnicity. Ethnicity, in fact, was not really a concept in its modern sense at the time of the psalm's composition. Rather, these little ones are the progeny of the evil spirit who is here being condemned. They are the sins, evil thoughts, and temptations placed in the minds and hearts of humanity that lead humans to destruction. These thoughts and temptations lead, for example, one people group to rejoice at the suffering of her neighbor. They are the source of all resentment and wickedness and violence. Just as Yahweh, the God of Israel, is the Blessed One par excellence who will bring justice to Satan for his wickedness and destruction, so also is the person blessed who resists and defeats Satan, not falling prey to him as did the Edomites of the sixth century BC.

Gigantomachy

IT IS A RELATIVELY WELL-KNOWN fact that the story of Noah's Flood found in Genesis 6—9 is paralleled in other ancient literature. The Epic of Gilgamesh is likely the most famous example, a version of the story that predates the writing of the biblical account by centuries. The story of the sinking of Atlantis is also widely known, though often not connected by modern people to the same theme of a previous advanced civilization destroyed by a flood. In truth, nearly every ancient culture on earth possesses some version of this story, based on a shared collective memory handed down through oral tradition. The version related in the Torah, then, is not so much imparting new information to readers, whether they be Israelites or from one of the nations; rather, it is asserting itself as the true account of what happened in this universally acknowledged event.

Even less well known than the universality of this flood story is the universality of other related stories found in Genesis, the Torah, and the historical books of the Hebrew Bible. One of these elements relates to the nature of the civilization that was destroyed by the Flood. The ancient world universally conceived this civilization to be advanced, and the source of that advancement was the revelation of divine secrets. In the Babylonian understanding, the origin of this knowledge was the seven sages, the *apkallu*, who revealed heavenly secrets to the antediluvian kings. In the Sumerian Kings List, each king before the coming of the Flood is described as having an apkallu as an advisor. After the Flood, the subsequent kings are said to be two-thirds apkallu. Those apkallu before the Flood who had revealed these secrets were punished by the gods through imprisonment in the abyss. Likely the most well-known parallel versions would be the Greek stories of Prometheus and the Titans.

The text of Genesis reflects the Israelite version of this story before the coming of Noah's Flood. The genealogy of Cain includes several elements. It is Cain who builds the first city, the Sumerian city of Eridu, which was believed to be the first in the world (Gen. 4:17–18). Cain's lineage produces the major elements of culture and technology (vv. 19–22). That line culminates in Lamech, a polygamous king who sings a song of his own glory and violent retribution (vv. 23–24). The corruption of the earth culminates, at the time of the Flood, with the intermingling of angelic beings with humanity (Gen. 6:1–4). This intermingling produces Nephilim, giants.

The Israelite traditions surrounding this event, reflected in the biblical text, are preserved in a more fully elaborated form in other literature. Chief among these is the Book of Enoch, commonly referred to as 1 Enoch, as well as texts like the Book of Jubilees, the Book of the Giants, and others. In these texts, the innovations of Cain's descendants are revealed by rebellious angelic beings who give to humanity technology and wisdom that they are not ready to receive. The rebellious beings revealed this knowledge with the intent of furthering humanity's descent into evil and self-destruction. In response to their rebellion, they were imprisoned in the abyss. The New Testament explicitly refers to their sin, punishment, and imprisonment (1 Pet. 3:19–20; 2 Pet. 2:4–9; Jude 6–7).

Genesis 6:1–4 describes the progeny produced at the culmination of this angelic rebellion as giants who are part divine and part human. This parallels the two-thirds divine, one-third human status of the kings after the deluge in the Sumerian Kings List. The most famous of these kings is Gilgamesh, who was likewise regarded as two-thirds divine. Gilgamesh's name not only is prominent in Babylonian history and religion but also was so associated with the giants that his name is preserved in the Book of the Giants at Qumran, found among the Dead Sea Scrolls, millennia after the composition of the Epic of Gilgamesh. Parallel figures, divine-human kings and demigods, abound as founder figures, culture heroes, and doers of great deeds throughout all ancient cultures, as implied by the biblical reference to them as "men of renown" (Gen. 6:4). These kings, historically, claimed to possess supernaturally revealed knowledge from before the Flood as part of their claim to authority. The most prominent of these groups in the ancient Near East were the Martu, the biblical Amorites, of whom Hammurabi is likely the most prominent member.

Likewise, there are near-universal traditions of giants and a war against them. In Greek stories, the giants were children of Gaea, the earth, brought forth to take revenge for the Titans after their imprisonment in Tartarus. Celtic stories describe the malformed Fomorians, who were part human and part faerie. Giants likewise feature prominently in Germanic and Old Norse stories as well as in the memory of Southeast Asian and even Meso-American cultures. In every case, these giants were monstrous and wicked beings who needed to be defeated by the most recent tier of gods and human beings, often working in tandem.

How should we understand the historical reality of these traditions? Most modern interpreters regard such stories as flights of fancy and silliness at best. At worst, they view these stories as a way of dehumanizing a people's enemies to justify retaliatory or even preemptive violence. To better understand this reasoning, it's worth pointing out that the term *giant* is not primarily a description of physical size in either the Hebrew/Aramaic or Greek roots. Here, the words being translated as "giant" are more akin to someone being a tyrant, bully, or thug. The shared cultural memory, then, is of a time when humans were materially and spiritually oppressed by such kings. The text of Genesis likewise casts the heroic figures of the founding stories of Israel's neighbors as wicked oppressors.

Modern interpreters often understand these stories, both in and outside Israel and the Scriptures, as describing a kind of divine/ human hybridization. It must be remembered that ancient people had no concept of DNA or genetics as such. Further, the designation as two-thirds divine, rather than having one divine and one human parent, means that the ancient understanding was not so simple. Idolatry and sexual immorality are closely linked in Israelite, Second Temple, and Christian traditions because they were closely linked in the ancient pagan world. Ritualized sexual activity with shrine and temple prostitutes, often enacted by the king, who was seen to be embodying the god, were common parts of the festal cycle in ancient cities. A child produced in such a circumstance would be seen to have two fathers—one a god, one a divine king—and a single human mother. There is evidence of this practice in the text of the Torah itself, where Og, one of the giant kings, is described as having a massive metallic bed (Deut. 3:8–11). These dimensions match that of a ritual bed found in the ziggurat temple of Etemenanki.

Within the pages of Scripture we find not only giant kings, demonic tyrants, and oppressors over the nations, but also giant clans and tribes. Here again, there is a tendency for modern interpreters to import notions of heredity and ethnicity. However, tribes and clans were not determined by these then-unknown concepts in the ancient world. Membership in these social units was defined ritually. In the case of ancient Israel, people were Israelites because they were circumcised or were the daughter or wife of a circumcised male, they ate the Passover, and they worshipped Yahweh, the God of Israel. Likely the most prominent non-ethnic Israelite of the Torah and the Book of Joshua is Caleb. At his first introduction in the text, Caleb is described as a Kenizzite (Num. 32:12). By the conclusion of the Book of Joshua, Caleb is not only a member but an elder of the tribe of Judah (Josh. 15:13).

Likewise, membership in one of these giant clans was determined not by DNA or ethnic features but by ritual. Such ceremonies involved not only the sexual immorality described above but also human sacrifice, reflected in the depiction of the giants in Israelite and Second Temple sources as consumers of human flesh (e.g., 1 Enoch 7:4–6). When Yahweh identifies and judges these clans within the Old Testament history, it is critically important that this factor of identity be taken into account. God does not render judgment based on the identity of one's father, or great-grandfather, or the clan's founder. The members of the clan were active participants in this ritual life, which constituted the clan as a social unit.

If a clan member repudiated these practices, he or she would need to leave the tribe and be integrated ritually, through rites of initiation, into another. Ancient people did not think of themselves first as individuals, then as members of various voluntary associations. A person's identity—who he or she was—was a function of the role played in the family, clan, tribe, or city. Abandoning one of these identities for a new one was to become a new person. Just as one example, the rituals for the incorporation of Canaanite women into Israel signify such a rebirth (Deut. 21:10–14).

This form of repentance was always available. A tribe or clan could be annihilated not only through acts of violence but through the assimilation of its members into another social unit. If all the

Amalekites died or were integrated into other tribes and clan units that didn't practice the same abominable rites, then the Amalekites as such would have been eradicated. The command to let no Amalekite live can be fulfilled either by the death of an Amalekite person or by that person continuing to live, but not as an Amalekite.

The Books of Numbers, Deuteronomy, and Joshua describe a gigantomachy, a war against the giant clans, directed by Yahweh and prosecuted by the descendants of Abraham. Though readers rarely peruse the genealogies of the latter portions of Genesis in detail, one of their major concerns is establishing the origin and identities of these clans, which will later come under judgment. The kings and elders of the giant clans are not only tyrants in the material, political sense but also, through the rituals they lead, bringing about spiritual, demonic oppression. These acts have had the effect of defiling the land itself, and, as was promised to Abraham, these clans will be removed to make way for his descendants to take possession of it. These descendants include not only the Israelites but the descendants of Ishmael, Esau, Ammon, and Moab. All these groups will be charged with maintaining the purity and holiness of the land as a condition of their continuing to dwell there.

The historical narrative of the Old Testament presents Israel not as the prime mover of this war against the giant clans but as the ones who bring it to completion. Before Israel arrived at the land of Canaan, the Moabites, the Ammonites, the Edomites, and even the Caphtorim had already driven the giant clans from their respective territories (Deut. 2:8–24).[3] Yahweh, having brought these Abrahamic peoples to their respective territory to render judgment against the giant clans then inhabiting it, has set up the paradigm for what

---

3   Interestingly, the Caphtorim are Cretans, in this case the biblical Philistines. That Greeks were somehow descended from Abraham is a tradition that arises later in the Christian Old Testament (see 1Mc 12:21).

Israel is about to be called upon to do. Already, most of the Rephaim, the Emim, the Zamzummim, the Avvim, the Horites, and many of the Amorites had been removed.

By the time of the war against the giant clans as described in Deuteronomy, Israel had already encountered one such clan, the Amalekites. Amalek appears in Esau's genealogy as the offspring of Esau's grandson and a concubine who is said to be the "sister of Lotan" (Gen. 36:12). Lotan is the name of one of the chiefs of the Horite giant clan. It is also the Canaanite form of the name of the chaos monster commonly transliterated as *Leviathan* in English. Not only does this lineage connect Amalek to a giant clan, but it also connects his conception to precisely the kind of demonic sexual immorality that produced the Nephilim in the first place.

The clan of Amalek had attempted to slaughter the nascent Israelite nation in the wilderness as they came to camp at Mount Sinai. Because Yahweh had descended upon Sinai, it had become the mountain of God, the place of His throne. The clan of Amalek laid siege not only to the Israelite people in the desert but also to the throne of the God of Israel Himself. In the battle that ensued, Moses stood on a high place and held out his arms, which granted victory to Israel. Because the Amalekites had dared attack Yahweh and His people, Amalek would be destroyed as a clan. They would suffer the same fate they had intended for Israel (Ex. 17:8–16).

As they prepared to enter Canaan, Israel faced another pair of giant foes: Sihon, the king of the Amorites, and Og, the king of Bashan (Deut. 2:26—3:22). Og's identity as a giant has already been described, as has the connection between the Nephilim and the Amorites. These are the first two brief battles of what will become a lengthy campaign described in the Book of Joshua, but the infamy of Og as the last of the Rephaim, the ancient giant kings, and Sihon as an Amorite gave great import to Yahweh's defeat of them on Israel's behalf. The defeat of these demonic foes is recounted repeatedly in the Old Testament, including twice in the Psalms (Ps. 136/135:11; 137/136:19–20). These psalms, and therefore the defeat of Og and Sihon, are still sung in the Orthodox Church as part of the Polyeleos.

God gives Israel specific instructions regarding the conquest of the land. Seven clans, the Hittites, Girgashites, Amorites, Canaanites, Perizzites, Hivites, and Jebusites, are to be completely destroyed (Ex. 23:23, 28; 33:2; 34:11; Deut. 7:1; 20:17; Josh. 3:10; 9:1; 24:11). He brings judgment against these giant clans for their unrepentant wickedness and corruption of the land. In all these commandments, which will involve the Israelites making war, it is Yahweh who presents Himself as the agent of the judgment of these clans. He is rendering His judgment and using Israel as the means of applying it, as He had used the waters of the Flood or the fire that fell on Sodom and Gomorrah. He is using Israel as He would later use Assyria and Babylon to bring judgment upon Israel and Judah for their wickedness.

Not only the devoted members of the giant clans but even their material possessions and livestock are considered to be *cherem*, "accursed" or "forbidden" (Deut. 7:26; 13:17; Josh. 6:17–18; 7:1–15; 22:20; 1 Sam./1Kg 15:21). Many English translations render this term as the clans and their possessions being placed "under the ban" or "devoted to destruction." Something being accursed is naturally the opposite of it being holy, but just as holy things are set apart, so also are the accursed things to be set apart so they can be destroyed. Because Israel's acts of war against these clans—and only against these clans—were Yahweh's judgment, He did not give them the spoils (Deut. 20:14–18). Having been corrupted by the wickedness of the giant clans, these objects were now unfit for any use. Israel had to maintain its holiness by holding itself apart from them.

While these clans are to be blotted out, Israel is strictly forbidden to pursue such total war against anyone else (Deut. 20:10–18). Other nations can enter into treaties and vassal relationships with Israel. Members of other tribes and clans and peoples can live among the Israelites as sojourners, and the Israelites are enjoined not to abuse or exploit them. Because of the ways of these giant clans, however, they cannot be allowed to live with or among Israel, lest Israelites begin to follow their ways and keep their ritual practices. Even if Israel does not participate in them, those practices taint, corrupt, and curse the land itself. Once Joshua and Israel have destroyed the Anakim, another name for the giant clans, the conquest is considered complete (Josh. 11:21–22). The final few remaining giant clan members escaped to Gaza, Gath, and Ashdod, three cities of the Philistines. Their presence and activities moved the Philistines from an instrument against the giant clans to an enemy of Israel.

It fell to David, the first king of his line from Judah, to bring the gigantomachy to its conclusion. In fact, Scripture portrays the completion of this warfare as a major component of his status as the head of the Messianic line. It is David who finally defeats and destroys the Amalekite clan (1 Sam./1Kg 30:16–18; 1 Chr. 4:43). David's first great exploit after his consecration as king was the defeat of the giant Goliath from the city of Gath, one of the survivors of Joshua's conquest (1 Sam./1Kg 17). David and his ranking commanders likewise killed the remaining members of Goliath's clan from among the Philistines (2 Sam./2Kg 21:19; 1 Chr. 20:5). The Philistines themselves are not eradicated, as they were not wholesale guilty of the ritual acts and wickedness of the giants.

The wars that Israel fought, beginning at Sinai, through Joshua's conquest, and David's early battles, are not acts of genocide or ethnic cleansing but are highly targeted acts of judgment in which Israel is used by God. They are aimed only at particular clans who have committed continued acts of demonic tyranny and wickedness, which have polluted the land and accumulated countless victims whose blood cries out for justice. Any clans who insist on continuing these ways must, therefore, perish. For the sake of these clans' past and future victims, they could not be allowed to continue.

Casting Out Demons

ALL TOO OFTEN, THE HEBREW Bible and the Christian Old Testament are not read in the way just described. Readers assume, on the contrary, that the warfare of the Old Covenant lacked a spiritual dimension, that they are merely accounts of obscure battles over territory, grievances, and prejudices. Any religious references in the text are presumed to be justifications after the fact for violent actions, resituating the decision to go to war as a divine one rather than a human calculation. At best, the texts are simply demythologized. Readers ignore references to supernatural elements, while those that jibe with a materialist worldview are taken literally. At worst, the text is rejected as having no value whatsoever.

When one turns to the New Testament, however, there is a great deal more clarity. A given reader may (or may not) accept, for example, the reality of demons, the phenomenon of demonic possession, or the supernatural nature of Christ's miracles. Yet wherever one falls on these topics, it is clear from the New Testament texts that the enemies of man that are spoken of and defeated by the power of Christ are evil spiritual forces. Christ and His apostles clearly taught love not only for one's neighbor but even for the enemy. Ire, vengeance, and wrath are clearly directed against sin, wickedness, and their agents.

Thus the shallow reading of the Old Testament contrasts sharply with the clear meaning of the New. Some solve this dilemma uncharitably by simply stating that the two Testaments within Scripture are opposed to each other. Others argue more charitably that some sort of transition has taken place with the coming of Christ. Those who take this approach, of the life of Christ representing a shift, describe it in various ways. Some take the approach that the Old Testament did indeed describe material realities, material warfare, nationalistic identity, and strife. Over against this, they read the New Testament as describing spiritual realities, spiritual warfare, and a larger sense of identity in Christ that supersedes the national identity of the Old Testament. The shift, then, could be described as "spiritualization," a sort of allegorical reading of the Old Testament built into the New. Depending on the view that an interpreter takes of the historical veracity of the Hebrew Bible, Old Testament places, personages, and events may be material pointers or symbols to a later spirituality, or they may be parables or otherwise fictional tales intended to communicate spiritual realities to "primitive" peoples.

The reading of the Christian Old Testament here described sees spiritual warfare as the overarching theme of the original texts. This reading is not an interpretive trick but is the meaning of the Old Testament in its original context. The meaning of the Old Testament, then, is in continuity with the clear meaning of the New Testament as it regards the enemies of humanity and the objects of Christian enmity and warfare. Read correctly, there is no disparity in the quality of teaching between the Testaments. Both describe historical events of spiritual import. Both describe spiritual warfare against rebellious spiritual powers who are the enemies of humanity. Both describe Yahweh, the God of Israel, as the one who grants victory over these foes. There being no dichotomy or disjuncture to be bridged, the proposed explanations become irrelevant and unnecessary. Those who wish, for other theological reasons, to maintain one of the alternative solutions, such as the allegorical nature of the Old Testament or the spiritualization of the New, must then argue in favor of some massive difference between the Testaments. They must create the problem for which they want to argue a solution.

Additionally, the New Testament itself makes the positive case for the continuity of its vision with that of the Old Testament on this particular set of points. This continuity begins with the simple fact that the commandment to "love your neighbor as yourself" is cited from the Book of Leviticus, from the Holiness Code in the Torah. The connection here is not merely symbolic or allegorical. Rather, it is literal. The enemies against whom imprecations are uttered and wars are made during the Old Covenant are the same rebellious, evil spirits against whom spiritual warfare is made in the New.

The synoptic Gospels—Matthew, Mark, and Luke—portray Christ, among other ways, as a new Joshua. The most obvious means of doing so is that Jesus has the same name as the Old Testament son of Nun. Beyond this, they portray Christ's mission as beginning with His Baptism by St. John the Forerunner. As Joshua led the people of Israel through the Jordan River to begin the conquest of the land from the dark spiritual forces who had claimed it, so also does Christ lead the people assembled by St. John through baptism in the Jordan into the land to retake it. Orthodox hymnography and iconography often refer to the Jordan parting at the time of Christ's Baptism, an event described by Joshua but not by the Gospel writers. This makes the early Christian interpretation of these events quite clear.

Demonic possession and exorcism at the hands of Christ and His disciples are commonplace in these three Gospels. This phenomenon is mentioned only narrowly in the Christian Old Testament and certainly lacks the prominence there that it takes in the Gospel accounts. Christ's authority over demons is a major element of His ministry and of the manifestation of His identity as the Messiah. The Judeans of the first century AD held a common belief as to the origin of these evil spirits who now possessed and afflicted the people of the land. They were considered to be the disembodied spirits of dead Nephilim—dead giants.[4]

---

4   For more on the origin and consistency of this belief within Judaism of the Second Temple period, see Archie Wright, *The Origin of Evil Spirits* (Minneapolis: Fortress Press, 2015).

While most of the spirits of the giants were condemned to the abyss in Sheol or Hades, Judeans believed that God allowed a certain number to remain within the world in order to torment the wicked and bring them to repentance. The exorcism stories of the Gospels frequently allude to this understanding. For example, demons accuse Christ of wanting to torment them or cast them into the abyss "before the time" (Matt. 8:29). The demons that Jesus exorcised are not only analogous to the giant clans of the Old Testament. Joshua, son of Nun, and Jesus Christ battled the same enemies in the same land to free the land and its people from their wickedness and oppression. Exorcisms by the apostles and in the history of the Church are the continuation of this spiritual warfare from the Old Testament.

Likewise, the demonic kings and princes who have captured the nations through idolatrous worship continue to be the enemies of the New Testament. As St. Paul says, "We do not wrestle against flesh and blood, but against the rulers, against the authorities, against the spiritual powers over this present darkness, against the spiritual forces of evil in the heavenly places" (Eph. 6:12). As St. Paul preaches the gospel of Jesus Christ, he not only is proclaiming the victory of Christ over these powers but is continuing that battle to reclaim the people of the pagan nations, whom they have enslaved. He speaks to the pagans whom he has brought to Christianity as ones who have been held captive by evil spiritual powers, from whom Christ has set them free (Gal. 4:3, 9; Col. 2:8, 20). Christ's commission, sending the apostles out into the world, is based on His having taken all authority in heaven and on earth. It is for this reason that the apostles are to go to all the nations, not only Judea, to baptize and make disciples (Matt. 28:18–20).

The New Testament, therefore, does not speak of a different spiritual reality than does the Old. It does not allegorize or spiritualize the latter. The New Testament texts speak of the same spiritual reality as the Old Testament. Christ's Incarnation, life, death,

81

Resurrection, and Ascension to be enthroned at the right hand of the Father do indeed represent a shift, but this is a shift of epoch or age, not of interpretation or meaning. Many of the promised judgments and victories of the previous age have now become a reality. History has progressed, as has the plan of God with Christ at its center. The times in which we live are different than those of the Old Testament. God, reality, and the plan of salvation, however, have not changed.

5

Holy War

W AR, OBVIOUSLY, INVOLVES VIOLENCE. THOUGH war is violence writ large throughout human history, war in the ancient world was particularly brutal. The ancient world lacked a concept of "war crimes." Within that world, the reader of Scripture is confronted with God's people waging war, often accompanied by massive death tolls. More troubling still, at times the people of Israel go to war at the direction of Yahweh. Particular leaders, including sometimes priests, are praised for violent actions against foreigners and other Israelites. A surface reading of many passages of the Old Testament could give the impression that God condones, commands, or even praises violent actions that today would be called atrocities.

Rather than promoting or glorifying warfare, as the religious cults of the war gods of the surrounding nations all too often did, Yahweh, the God of Israel, places barriers in the way of violence. People groups, tribes, and nations will come into conflict with each other, and that conflict will erupt into violence; this is the reality of the present world. In the ancient Near East, victory and the resulting spoils were the primary virtues to be pursued when making war. Israel, by contrast, was to practice holy war.

Mentioning the phrase "holy war" evokes images of atrocities committed during the Crusades in the name of Islam and Christianity. Yet the concept has a much longer history and is present in the Hebrew Scriptures. At the same time, however, Old Testament concepts of holy war are unique. What distinguishes a war as holy, according to biblical understandings, is not the particular cause or justification (e.g., waging a war in order to gain converts) but rather whether the nation or military waging war remains faithful to the Law's commandments concerning proper conduct during warfare. Later Byzantine emperors and others appealed to this concept of holy war in the Scriptures. War was not total or exempt from rules, and the violation of certain biblical norms constituted war crimes.

This notion of holy war contrasts with the nations that neighbored Israel in the ancient Near East. The belief was universal—even among the Hebrews—that the gods were involved in warfare. When one nation waged war on another, their gods likewise entered into conflict. The gods were members of their communities, the pinnacle of a hierarchy that included every member of that locale. The ritual lives of communities were centered on strengthening and unifying the bonds between spiritual powers and their human community, as well as ties within the community.

Success in war, therefore, involved sacrifice, not necessarily because the gods were puppet masters controlling events on earth, but because to find victory, the community would need to persuade their gods to engage in battle against their opponent. The gods did not determine events in a fatalistic way; rather, they actively engaged in combat against other divine beings to determine superiority. To make things more complicated, gods were known to defect, either out of displeasure with their own community or because of favor curried by the opponent. After such a battle, particularly if the victory was decisive, it was natural to conclude that the gods of the victor were superior to those of the defeated. Most often, the gods of the conquered were integrated into the lower level of the victor's pantheon. But this was not the case with Israel. A major theme in the Hebrew prophets was emphasizing that Babylon's defeat of Judah did not translate to Marduk's defeat of Yahweh, but rather that Yahweh chastened His people by allowing King Nebuchadnezzar to overtake them.

For these pagan nations, however, the objective was to gain divine favor, which was secured not through the moral state of the people but rather through properly performing rituals, building temples, and performing other acts of worship in service of the gods. Although the ancient people of Judah and Israel often related to Yahweh in these pagan terms, Yahweh rejected such efforts and was interested solely in the faithfulness of His people. He was continuously loyal, despite the manifold sins of Israel and Judah and their outright rebellion against His commandments. Nonetheless, Israel continued to make sacrifices at the temple and the northern shrines apace—attempting to gain Yahweh's aid through these more pagan, magical means—but they were unsuccessful. In fact, Yahweh ultimately told His people to cease offering sacrifices as long as their hearts remained unrepentant and they continued to do evil (Is. 1:11–20; 66:2–3; Hos. 8:11–13; Mic. 6:7–8).

For Yahweh to fight on His people's behalf required their faithful obedience. This included worshipping Him alone as well as following the moral commands regarding sexual morality, the care of the poor and the weak, repentance, and holiness. The most important commands in this context, however, were those concerning warfare itself. The idea of any sort of moral code applied within warfare was a massive break with the general understanding of the ancient world. The ancient Near East conceived of one's home city and the world of war as two separate spheres governed by radically different rules. To state it perhaps more bluntly, there were no rules in the world of war— massacre, rape, and mass enslavement were acceptable. There simply was no notion of "war crimes." Indeed, the realization that there ought to be limits and safeguards in war largely evolved from the Christian appropriation of Old Testament understandings of holy war.

Ritual Warfare

THE ARMIES OF ANCIENT ISRAEL and Judah could be successful in battle only if Yahweh led them into battle. This attitude reflects a continuity with broader spiritualized views of warfare common to the ancient Near East, yet it also signals discontinuity between Israel's understanding and that of her neighbors. Or, at least, Israel and Judah ought to have conducted themselves differently in warfare than their neighbors. Yet it is commonly, albeit incorrectly, assumed that any event or deed Scripture contains is an implicit endorsement of it.

The books that comprise the Christian Old Testament are ancient texts, but this does not mean that they are somehow primitive or incapable of nuanced communication. There are times when the texts explicitly pass judgment on persons and their actions, such as the repeated refrain of the Book of Judges that "in those days there was no king, and each one did what was right in his own eyes" or its identification of nearly all the kings of Israel and Judah as wicked men. At other times, however, divine disapproval is signaled in more subtle ways, for example, through divine silence or the portrayal of the negative consequences of certain actions.

But perhaps the most important, if often neglected, way the Scriptures indicate divine judgment is simply through context. The Hebrew Scriptures and the additional material that makes up the Christian Old Testament were not written together all at once; nor were they written in complete isolation and compiled only later. Instead, the many disparate books and texts emerged from a coherent tradition that was gathered, expanded, and reshaped over time.

The historical books of the Old Testament, those that follow the Torah—namely Joshua, Judges, and the books Samuel and

Kings—are often called by scholars the "Deuteronomistic History." They chronicle the history of Israel and Judah but make no pretense to modern concepts of historical objectivity. Instead, they offer Israel's history from a distinct perspective: the God of Israel's teaching as found in the Torah, particularly Deuteronomy. Many of the psalms of David received later superscriptions connecting them to events in the life of David, as described in those historical books.[1] The prophecies of the Hebrew prophets were given at specific points in the history of Israel and Judah. They are not prophetic visions disassociated from events in the ancient world. Those prophecies also describe judgment and blessings based on the promised blessings and curses of the Torah.

It is, therefore, not only acceptable but necessary to compare actions and events in the Scriptures to preceding elements of the scriptural tradition. This is true even when the biblical text itself does not explicitly make such a comparison. The text of the Books of Kings is continuously and tacitly comparing later kings to David, though it makes this comparison explicit only a few times (e.g., 1 Kin./3Kg 14:7–10). Polygamy within the Old Testament era was turning out to have terrible consequences for families in the narrative when compared to the original institution of marriage between the first created humans. The reader is thus invited to judge Israel and Judah's actual historical religious behavior against the worship and ritual practice that Yahweh, the God of Israel, commanded in the Torah.

It is incontrovertible that for most of their respective histories, Israel and Judah approached warfare in the same way as their neighbors. They sought to gain favor with their God over and against the gods of their opponents and to do so through sacrificial rituals, which they all too often viewed in magical terms. They sought to use the ark

---

1   These superscriptions begin with Psalm 3.

of the covenant in battle, for instance, as a sort of talisman to guarantee victory—with disastrous results (1 Sam./1Kg 4). Rather than seeking the will of God, they often used violence to impose their own national will, the will of the human king.

As already discussed in the previous chapter, the God of Israel had stipulated which land belonged to which nation, tribe, and clan of Israel. He had given direction regarding whom Israel was to wage war against and how total that war ought to be. This meant two things after the partial conquest of the land under Joshua, which was hindered by Israel's faithlessness. First, the people were to seek the will of God regarding warfare before engaging in battle. The directives regarding the conquest of Canaan had been given clearly through Moses, but going forward, Israel needed to inquire of God. Second, when warfare was approached correctly, Israel was to engage in it through ritual means to reinforce the reality that God was fighting not alongside His people but for them in the sense that He was granting victory. It was not a result of their might or stratagem. The victory belonged to Yahweh, and He distributed the fruits of that victory to His people.

As mentioned, the end of the Book of Joshua left the conquest, at least as it had been described in the Torah, incomplete in certain regards. Because of their faithlessness to God's promises, several of the tribes had failed to take possession of their inheritance. Small groups of remaining giant clan members had taken shelter in the cities of the Philistines, who had given them aid and comfort. The remnants of the Amalekite giant clans were also active at the borders of Israel's territory. It was therefore still within the revealed will of God that these aspects of the conquest and His judgment be brought to their conclusion. This held importance for only a brief period at the beginning of the Israelite monarchy, however. Even during this period when David brought the destruction of the Amalekites to its conclusion, there were other issues of warfare and battle that fell outside of these commandments of the Torah.

Just as the conquest of Canaan was about the Israelites participating in God's will in the world and executing His judgment, so also any future war they waged was to be rooted in obedient participation in the will of God. They were to offer themselves as instruments of God to bring about justice and thereby peace. This ran contrary to the dominant approach to war throughout the rest of the world. War had largely been an effort to enlist the divine in the cause of some human tribe—for the gods to do the tribe's will. This effort took the form of using ritual, particularly sacrifice, to cajole deities into taking sides. In the modern, materialist world, nations use rhetoric and persuasion, which insist that God is on "our" side, whoever a particular "us" might be conceived to be over against an outside "them."

Determining what God willed on the question of going to battle was not merely a subjective matter. It was not the stuff of political entities in the modern world, who gain adherents by claiming God's will to justify expanding their territory or attacking a neighboring country. An opponent may make the same argument to legitimize the opposite position. Instead, the God of Israel had enacted multiple measures by which elders, tribal leaders, and later kings could determine His will in such cases.

The first of these was Yahweh's prophets. The Torah itself promises a succession of prophets after Moses. Yahweh explicitly established the institution of the prophet within Israel as an alternative to various forms of divination (Deut. 18:9–22). He would speak through His prophet, therefore forbidding the types of ritual forecasting of the future common among Israel's neighbors. He also included in this injunction the means of discerning who is and is not truly the prophet of Yahweh, anticipating future false claims to that office.

Prior to a battle, it was typical in the ancient world outside of Israel to offer sacrifices to the deities—and possibly the deities of one's opponents in order to persuade them to switch sides. As part of the sacrificial ritual, a particular type of priest would "read" the entrails of the animal, usually particular organs, according to certain signs perceptible in them.[2] Based on which of these signs were present or absent, the priest would then claim to have ascertained whether the sacrifice was accepted and whether the battle would be successful. Presumably, in most ancient battles, both sides had come to the same determination. Other practices involved consulting oracles—humans possessed by spirits, through whom those spirits would communicate—or the summoning of the spirits of the dead to give knowledge. Saul, the king of Israel's final act of sinful rebellion, rejected Yahweh's prophet and instead resorted to the latter ritual of necromancy (1 Sam./1Kg 28).

Not only was the prophet available as a means for Israel and Judah to inquire of God, but He would take the initiative to send His prophet to declare His will. There are a number of examples of this happening before battles (e.g., 1 Kin./3Kg 22:13–28). To reveal the will of God in all the various aspects of Israelite and Judahite life can also serve as an overarching description of the ministry of the prophets in general. Their status as servants and messengers distinguishes the prophets of Yahweh from the prophets of other nations, who were, typically, independent operators who performed certain spiritual services for profit. Balaam is the prime biblical example of such a pagan prophet (Num. 22:1–20). If the shepherds of Israel had followed the Torah's means for establishing the identity of Yahweh's prophet and had followed his words, there would never have been ambiguity regarding God's will in any matter, especially so weighty a matter as war.

In cases where some sort of ambiguity might exist, God's will would be communicated through the Urim and Thummim, two stones kept in the ephod of the high priest. It is not clear precisely

---

2   This practice of reading the organs of an animal at its sacrifice is known as
     extispicy.

how these two stones were used to make such a determination. The mentions of their use in the biblical text imply that this was at least similar to the casting of lots. Thus the high priest at any given time was a second source of guidance along with the prophet or prophets. The Urim and Thummin also restricted a whole other set of divination-related practices to one ritual performed by one priest in Israel.

One of the most prominent references to the use of the Urim and Thummim in the Scriptures relates directly to the relationship between Joshua and Eleazar, the high priest (Num. 27:12–23). Key to Joshua's ability to succeed Moses as leader of Israel is his access to Eleazar, Aaron's son, to aid him in determining the will of the God of Israel—especially in deciding whether to go to battle. The "going out and coming in" language of Numbers is typical language used to refer to engaging in or declining a battle.

This same language is used in 1 Samuel/1 Kingdoms 8 in the people's later demand for a king. In the modern period, this text has often been misinterpreted to mean that it was somehow sinful for Israel to have a human king. Yet Deuteronomy 17:14–20 is clear that this was not the case—Israel, after all, had a single human leader at her inception, with Moses and later Joshua. Rather, the sin in view is the rejection of God's leadership in war in favor of a human king, like those of the surrounding nations, who would lead Israel into battle (1 Sam./1Kg 8:19–20). Though Israel had possessed single human leaders, as had individual tribal units during the period of the Judges, it was clear that Yahweh—not any human authority—led them into battle and granted victory. Israel was demanding a human leader who himself would lead and win victories, even if this was against Yahweh's will (1 Sam./1Kg 8:10–18).

This demand for a human king comes immediately after the temporary loss of the ark of the covenant in battle to the Philistines (1 Sam./1Kg 4). Here the Israelites go out to meet the Philistines in battle and are defeated (v. 2). Since the Israelites do not know why they were defeated, it is apparent they had not inquired of God before heading forth into battle (v. 3). Yet rather than seeking out the will of Yahweh through the prophet or the high priest, they surmise of their own accord that if they carry the ark of the covenant into battle with them, they will become undefeatable (v. 4). Despite this, they were defeated resoundingly (v. 10). Their defeat is portrayed in the Scripture as the result of their attempt to manipulate God through ritual rather than submitting to His will.

The ritual element of carrying the ark into battle was intended for precisely the opposite purpose. It was not a magical object to coerce Yahweh into conferring victory on those who possessed it. Rather, the ritual was intended to reinforce to Israel, as she went into battle, that it was Yahweh who was fighting for her and to whom the victory belonged and that they were serving Him with their efforts (Num. 4; 10:33–35; Josh. 3:3–17; 4:5–18; 6:4–13). Carrying the ark was a ritual of obedience to Him, not one that compelled Him to do their will. In various other military circumstances, God acted to demonstrate to Israel this same truth by other means, as at the fall of Jericho, the winnowing of Gideon's army (Judg. 7:1–8), and the deliverance from the Assyrian siege (2 Kin./4Kg 19:35–37). Warfare, for Israel, was ritualized as a religious act of obedience to Yahweh, thus removing it from the realm of human will and tribalism.

Yet Israel ultimately failed to grasp this deeper dimension of war, leading to consistent defeat on the battlefield. This in turn led to kings being instituted as leaders in battle. The warfare that takes place throughout the period of the divided monarchies of Israel and Judah, then, is not representative of holy war as Yahweh had established it but rather signifies a critique of those commands. As described in the Scriptures, the Torah's prescribed practice of holy war existed only in the days of Moses and Joshua and was lost throughout the rest of Israelite history.

The ritual approach to warfare was not recovered until after the conversion of St. Constantine. One of the greatest signs of the veracity of his religious conversion was the immediate action he took in relation to pagan sacrifice. Even in the early fourth century, the Roman military practiced the offering of sacrifices to the gods to ensure success in battle. Following his turn to Christ, St. Constantine abolished these pagan sacrifices before combat and instead brought in Christian priests to celebrate the Eucharist. Although the Eucharist is a sacrifice, it is not one designed to gain favor with or manipulate the Holy Trinity. Rather, it is purifying and sanctifying. The sacrament is aimed not at changing or manipulating God but at cleansing the human partakers. Saint Constantine's change, then, represents a shift from seeking to align divine might with a human cause to seeking to align oneself and those under one's authority to the will and work of God in the world.

The Laws of War

FOR ISRAEL'S NEIGHBORS, WAR EXISTED as a different world than that of hearth and home. The city was the domain of the king and therefore was subject to his decrees and justice, as was the countryside, at least as far as he could extend his will through the military. In the succession of ancient empires, one great king might extend his will over other vassal kings, again through violence or its threat. This had several consequences. The regions between cities, even along the roads, were subject to lawlessness and assault, and travelers were often forced to defend themselves. There were no police or even military patrols along most roads. When troop movements occurred, they were more concerned with accomplishing their mission and protecting themselves than hearing the pleas of strangers and wanderers of the roads. A resident alien or sojourner who was not a citizen of a given city or region did not have any "rights" or any recourse for ill treatment there beyond violent revenge exacted by his clan, tribe, or city if they were able.

In the context of war, this meant that there was no law in battle, only the application of superior force and violence to bring about victory. One party's victory in war was itself proof of that party's superior virtue. Winning was seen as a virtue in and of itself, and being a victim or loser was something to be despised, not protected or aided. In the closing days of the Roman Republic, Cicero famously said, "*inter arma enem silent leges*" (in war, the laws are silent). This saying did not indicate merely a benign absence of law code or a temporary suspension of portions of Roman law. This meant that what was considered horror and atrocity in typical circumstances was commonplace in war and that these events, which would otherwise shock, were of no importance.

Examples of this principle exist even today, the most obvious being murder. While killing is strictly forbidden by all societies in most circumstances, it is the very stuff of war. In the ancient world, however, what was considered normal in warfare extended far beyond taking the lives of fellow combatants fighting for the other side and included the indiscriminate killing of men, women, and children. It was common practice to massacre the entire populations of cities who refused to surrender. These killings were not mere summary executions; they often involved torture and hideous displays of brutality designed to intimidate future opponents.

Assyrian kings were particularly graphic, boasting of the piles of decapitated heads built separately for men, women, and children, as well as the display of other body parts of slaughtered victims. Slaves were taken en masse for purposes of both forced labor and sexual abuse. As ancient militaries lacked any real concept of consent, rape in ancient warfare was just one more form of violence to be leveled against the enemy. When Julius Caesar returned victorious from the conquest of Gaul, the Roman people proudly celebrated him for having killed one million Gauls and enslaved one million more.

The Torah, then, represents a sharp contrast in its view of warfare to anything else in the ancient world. As part of His instruction to newborn Israel, Yahweh gave strict commandments both for when Israel was allowed to go to war and how Israel had to conduct herself while engaged in combat. Not only were the commandments of the Torah not suspended in time of war; additional commandments, particular to warfare and the taking of spoils, came into effect during these periods. Yet the Scriptures are explicit that Israel did not keep these commandments regarding war any better than they kept the others—Israel's eventual destruction and Judah's later exile are both the result of God's judgment after these commandments were violated. One cannot attribute the disobedient actions of Israel to God, whose law they have violated. In fact, Yahweh brought justice for these violations, including war crimes.

A nexus of the commandments regarding warfare in the Torah is found in Deuteronomy 20. Fronting these commandments is a ritual commandment aimed at the reality that Israel is acting in response to the will of God, not out of national interest. The text predicts future battles during which Israel is likely to find herself outnumbered and overpowered, in a material sense, by her enemies. This pronouncement is a ritual act because God calls a priest, rather than a king or war leader, to speak to the people and tell them that it is Yahweh, their God, who leads them into battle to fight for them against their enemies (vv. 2–4). This is not only a reminder. This truth—that it is Yahweh who leads and who gives victory—is the basis for the commandments that follow. As God of Israel, He has the authority both to establish conditions for His leadership and blessing and to enforce these conditions by not granting victory or not accompanying Israel into battle at all if they do not keep these commandments.

The first set of commandments deals not with the conduct of war but with a preceding issue: the composition of Israel's army. Because it is God who goes into battle and brings victory, having a greater quantity of soldiers than the enemy has is not necessary. This understanding goes beyond the proclamation that Israel should not be afraid if outnumbered. Ancient warfare was brutal and produced incredibly high rates of casualties. In a literal sense, it consisted of thousands of armored men with sometimes crude weapons beating each other to death over the course of days. Ancient technology, such as trained archers and chariots, could provide significant advantages to one side or the other. Nevertheless, in most cases, victory essentially boiled down to which side possessed the most forces and could therefore withstand the most casualties without being forced to surrender or retreat.

The power of God is greater than horses, chariots, and men-at-arms. Because masses of troops are then not needed, forced enlistment is forbidden—there is no need to draft men against their will. Before the army is officially set in order under commanders, any soldier who has recently begun an agrarian venture, or has gotten engaged, or is simply fearful and fainthearted at the prospect of battle, is allowed to leave (Deut. 20:5–9). The king and his generals must believe in the priest's proclamation to allow this. If they are confident that what God has said is true, they will have no difficulty allowing men under these circumstances to leave their assembled forces.

Israel was forbidden to undertake wars with the intention of expanding their territory beyond that granted to them by God. The only exception to this rule was the giant clans of the land of Canaan described in the previous chapter, who are once again listed in Deuteronomy (vv. 16–18). Even when Israel was making war within the larger framework of wars commanded by God or defensive war, she was required to, at every city, offer peace (v. 10). Even once war had begun, each battle was a last resort. If a city had either instigated a war or lay within the land Yahweh gave Israel and then surrendered, the inhabitants could be placed under vassalhood to Israel, paying tribute and entering into bondservant relationships (v. 11).

If a given city refused peace, however, Israel was allowed to lay siege. Unlike the tactics used in sieges against cities in the ancient Near East before this, however, failing to accept this final peace offering still did not give Israel license to unleash total war. Although the Israelite army was allowed to make war and even to kill, if necessary, the men of the city who constituted its military, they were not allowed to kill women and children (vv. 13–14). Neither were they permitted to slay the livestock or damage the land and its fruitfulness. This latter decree went so far as to forbid Israel from destroying fruit trees when searching for lumber to use for siegeworks (vv. 19–20). Only trees that did not produce food could be cut for this purpose.

Within ancient warfare, women were especially vulnerable. In most ancient cultures, with a few notable exceptions, women were neither skilled in nor allowed to participate in warfare. If they were taken as captives following the siege of a city, the fate of female prisoners was particularly dire. It was not uncommon for women facing capture to take their own lives and those of their children to prevent the violence that they knew was about to take place. Deuteronomy 21 gives commandments aimed at protecting women and children from a victorious Israelite army. An Israelite man could choose to take a woman from a captured city as his wife (21:10–14). An Israelite warrior cannot, however, take her as a concubine or sex slave, and if she is not taken as a wife, she is granted her freedom (v. 14). The commandments here lay out a process of cutting her hair, changing her clothes, and mourning her parents as if they had died—ritual enactments of disassociating herself from her people and becoming an Israelite. This process culminates in her marriage to a circumcised Israelite male and, therefore, becoming a full member of the people of Israel.

As cliché as it may sound, the differences between how Israel and its neighbors were called to conduct war are night and day. These differences begin, first and foremost, with the idea that there were commandments, rules, and laws that governed the conduct of men in war. The Torah protects the weak and innocent victims of war from the victors. Its commandments even protect the environment, the creation itself, from the ravages of human conflict. Far from the Old Testament allowances for warfare being some kind of primitive embarrassment, the Torah's commandments in this area would go on to form the basis for concepts of human rights, international law, and compacts like the Geneva Conventions.

Zealotry and the New Testament

IN THE OLD TESTAMENT, THE priesthood—at least in its initial stages—was generally seized by force, effectively being a reward for manslaughter. This simple fact confronts any careful reader of the Old Testament in general and the Torah in particular. The tendency produced an entire tradition of zealotry within the Old Testament that continued into the New Testament period. Simply defined in this context, zealotry is the idea that acts of violence, even the killing of other human persons, are not only allowed but required in defense of that which is holy and pure. This idea has been (wrongly) appealed to and applied throughout Christian history to defend everything from the Spanish Inquisition to the Crusades to witch-hunting. How ought this violence in defense of the sacred be understood?

In the earliest phase of biblical history, the patriarchal period recorded in the Book of Genesis and reflected in Job, there was not an established priesthood per se. For the most part, sacrifices were offered by fathers and heads of families. Abraham, Isaac, Jacob, Job, and others offered sacrifices on behalf of themselves and their families without being part of a priestly order or separate priestly tribe or clan. The major exception to this is the figure of Melchizedek, who appears briefly in the narrative of Abraham's life (Gen. 14:17–24). Melchizedek is a priest-king in typical ancient fashion. As the king of a city, he is seen as the father of all its people. His priesthood is, therefore, actually an extension of, rather than an exception to, the general rule.

This situation prevailed among Abraham's descendants until the time of the Exodus. Moses's father-in-law, Jethro, is a priest of God Most High and serves his extended family and clan as both leader and priest (Ex. 3:1). He continues to fulfill this role even after the Exodus and the birth of Israel (Ex. 18:1–12). The development of the priesthood as distinct from the role of leader, judge, and later the king was an anomaly in the history of Israel that distinguished the nation from most of her neighbors. Certainly, the prohibition of leaders and kings from performing priestly functions was unique. The reunion of these offices in the Person of Christ and the formation of a royal priesthood in the New Testament is not itself strange (Heb. 7:1–17; 1 Pet. 2:9). This restoration is the removal of a preceding anomaly.

The violence surrounding the initiation of the priesthood and priestly orders is a facet of the severing of these two roles. Israel did not perceive a need for a priestly class that would lead to the question, "Who is it who will fill this role?" Rather, God took away the responsibilities and privileges of the priesthood from individuals and gave them over to a separate priesthood as an act of judgment against those from whom they were taken. Typically, in these episodes recorded in Scripture, the priesthood is given to the ones who act in judgment against those who have abused the priestly role. The injustice and wickedness of priests are addressed, and those who deal with this injustice and restore the proper order receive those responsibilities in their stead.

This judgment begins with Moses himself. When called by Yahweh, the God of Israel, to lead and deliver Israel from Egypt, Moses responds with a series of excuses grounded not in humility but in general reticence and fear (Ex. 4:10–13). In response, God takes a portion of his authority from him and gives it to his brother, Aaron (vv. 14–17). Moses further complicates the matter by returning to Jethro rather than traveling to Egypt as commanded and by failing to circumcise himself and his son (vv. 24–26). Moses's recalcitrance was so great that Yahweh is said to have been prepared to kill him. His own wife, Zipporah, stepped in and fulfilled his responsibilities to atone for his sin. Because Moses failed in his ritual responsibilities, his priestly authority was taken from him and given to Aaron.

Aaron eventually became the first high priest, with his sons serving as priests (Lev. 8:1–36).

The tribe of Levi is known to have been the priestly tribe for ancient Israel and Judah. Moses and Aaron were Levites, as were the priesthoods of both the later Jerusalem temple and many of the false and pagan shrines established by disobedient Israel. When landholdings were assigned to the tribes and clans of Israel, the Levites received no land but rather had Yahweh as their inheritance (Josh. 18:7). Rather than being responsible for working a parcel of land to provide for themselves and their families, the Levites would receive portions of the offerings brought to the God of Israel at the tabernacle and later temple. This assignment of the priesthood to the Levites did not take place at the time of the division of the land under Joshua. It occurred earlier as an act of judgment.

Aaron received the role of the high priest, which had been taken from Moses, but this did not remove priestly responsibilities from the elders, fathers, and leaders of the various tribes and clans of Israel. They had, after all, not participated in Moses's disobedience. The elders retained these responsibilities at the time of the Exodus and immediately afterward. While Moses met with Yahweh atop Mount Sinai, nascent Israel took part in her first great act of rebellion, the worship of the golden calf. This idolatrous worship was led by Aaron (Ex. 32:1–5), but it was not purely his work. The plurality of the elders of Israel took part in the idolatrous sacrifices and incorporated sexual immorality (v. 6).

Idolatry and sexual immorality are sins that bring curse and corruption upon the land itself. The God of Israel informs Moses that for these sins, the people must be removed and that He will begin again by bringing forth a people from Moses (vv. 7–10). Moses intercedes, and the nation is not destroyed, but it still falls to him, as the leader of the people, to reestablish God's justice when he descends the mountain. This begins with a confrontation with Aaron (vv. 15–24). Even as Moses was taking action with Aaron regarding his sin, the people were continuing in their debauchery (v. 25). This ongoing, unrepentant rebellion jeopardized not only those participating but the entire community that had come into the presence of the holy God. Action had to be taken.

To assist him in putting an end to the rebellion, Moses calls out to ask who is on the side, not of Moses himself, but of Yahweh, the God of Israel. It is the Levites who respond (v. 26). Moses thereby offered peace and his intercessions (vv. 30–34) to all the people. Those who were hardened in their rebellion and refused to respond, deliberately taking sides against the God who had redeemed them and brought them to that place, had to be removed from the community. Their violent resistance and refusal of repentance was met with force by Moses and the Levites, who then killed a great many of the men who had been given the role of leadership and priesthood over their clans and families. In return, Yahweh gave those responsibilities to the Levites, who had proven loyal and zealous for His justice (v. 29).

Later, a similar act of rebellion unfolded at Peor. On the verge of entering the Promised Land of Canaan, Israel again fell into idolatry and related sexual immorality at the high place there to Baal (Num. 25:1–4). Moses gave an order to his elders and fellow leaders of Israel that this could not be allowed and that those who remained in this rebellion and refused repentance must be cut off from among their tribes and clans (v. 5). Despite this proclamation of the life-and-death seriousness of this rebellion, a man of Israel not only continued in this rebellion but flaunted it before the very gates of the tabernacle (v. 6). In response to the flagrance of this rebellious act, Phinehas, the grandson of Aaron, took up a spear and put the Israelite man and the ritual prostitute of Baal to death (vv. 7–8). Yahweh responds to Phinehas's action by making his family line the high priestly line of Israel in perpetuity (vv. 10–13).

This religious fervor to defend and preserve the holiness of God's presence and to protect the people from the consequence of its violation became known as zeal. The zeal to preserve sacred space, to make atonement for sin and protect the people, to maintain the honor and glory of Israel's God is the stuff of priesthood itself. Phinehas, in particular, would be held up as a model. It is this zeal that would later inspire the Maccabees in their revolt against the Seleucid Greek king who had desecrated Yahweh's temple (1Mc 2:1–14). By the first century AD, factions and coalitions of zealots planned violent insurrection against the Roman Empire, which controlled Judea. These insurrections would culminate in the Jewish revolts that ended with the destruction of the temple in AD 70 and the city of Jerusalem entire in AD 135. Two of Christ's twelve disciples are identified as members of zealot groups.[3]

The New Testament does not repudiate this tradition. Christ Himself, in His purification of the temple in Jerusalem, is said to

---

3   The obvious disciple is St. Simon the Zealot (Matt. 10:4; Mark 3:18; Luke 6:15; Acts 1:13). The Judas who betrayed Jesus is identified with the surname Iscariot (Matt. 10:4; 26:14; Mark 3:19; 14:10; Luke 6:16; 22:3; John 6:71; 12:4; 13:2, 26). This surname seems to identify him as a member of the Sicarii, a particularly violent zealot group known for assassinating Roman officials. That it is he who ends up collaborating with the Romans to kill the Messiah is a deliberate irony in the Gospels.

have fulfilled Psalm 69/68:9, "Zeal for Your house has consumed me" (John 2:13–17). Immediately following this episode, Christ redirects the understanding of zeal from a physical space to be protected with violence to His own person, which will suffer violence (vv. 18–20). The temple is now His own body (v. 21).

Saint Paul, likewise, who in his zeal was persecuting Christ Himself, does not repudiate zeal itself, but zeal not according to knowledge (Rom. 10:2). For St. Paul, the Holy Spirit now dwells within every Christian in the way He formerly resided in the temple, making them sacred and holy (1 Cor. 6:19). This holiness and the honor of the Spirit must be defended and protected zealously. Saint Paul goes so far as to use metaphors of doing violence to oneself in defense of this purity (1 Cor. 9:27). The restoration of the royal priesthood to all faithful Christians requires zeal and even ruthlessness in pursuit of both holiness and purity.

Problem Passages

THIS BOOK HAS SO FAR focused on themes that govern how we approach violence in the Scriptures, particularly the Old Testament. Before concluding, however, let us address several "problem passages" of Scripture that have particular bearing on this discussion, yet are prone to misunderstanding or even deliberate mischaracterization. Because of their ubiquity in anti-Christian polemic and in Christian concern, these texts warrant individual consideration.

Elisha and the She-Bears

ONE PASSAGE COMMONLY CITED AS an example of unjustified violence in the Hebrew Scriptures involves the prophet Elisha (2 Kin./4Kg 2:23–25). In this passage, as it is often depicted by skeptics or others who take issue with it, a small group of children make fun of Elisha—particularly his baldness—while he is traveling. In response, he curses them, and Yahweh sends two she-bears out of the woods who proceed to kill forty-two of the children who had mocked

105

him. The idea that God would massacre children at all—let alone for poking fun at someone—is troubling, to say the least, yet the above understanding is problematic on several accounts. First, it is based on a misleading translation of several key words. Second, it is taken out of its context within the narrative of the succession from Elijah to Elisha as Yahweh's chief prophet. Finally, it misunderstands the jeering targeted at Elisha. Let's explore these points carefully. When properly translated and understood, the story of these few verses takes on quite a different tone.

It is common not only in popular presentations of the story but even in most English translations to translate the word describing the identity of the mockers as "children," "boys," or "youths." This translation renders some elements of the story confusing. For example, this would mean that Elisha encountered a random mob of more than forty-two children descending the road from the city of Bethel. It is difficult at best to conceive of the situation in ancient Israel that would have produced such an encounter. Even now, finding forty-two unaccompanied children walking down the highway between cities would be strange, let alone in ancient Israel, where such roads were essentially lawless and filled with dangers. More importantly, however, the Hebrew term in question, na'ar (plural na'arim), is much more multifaceted and does not strictly connote young children.

For example, within the Greek Old Testament tradition, the word na'ar is translated in various contexts by sixteen different Greek words. Many of these usages could be brought under the general category of "young man." Just as "young man" can be used in a variety of ways in English, so also can the Hebrew term. Someone from childhood into his twenties could be referred to as a "young man" in English without it seeming odd. It could even be used as a pejorative in the context of putting a person behaving arrogantly back into his proper place.

One very common usage of na'ar is as a reference to a royal court official.[1] For example, one Ziba, who oversees the interests of Saul's grandson, is described as a na'ar (2 Sam./2Kg 16:2). We are told earlier in the text that this "young man" had fifteen sons (2 Sam./2Kg 9:10). At the battle of Michmash, Jonathan, Saul's son, brings with him his armor bearer, who fights alongside him and helps him kill more than twenty of the enemy in hand-to-hand combat (1 Sam./1Kg 14:1–14). This armor bearer is called a na'ar. In 2 Samuel/2 Kingdoms 2:12–16, a battle begins with a skirmish between twelve na'arim commanded by Avner and twelve commanded by Joab. It seems unlikely at best that these two generals watched children fight before engaging themselves. The prophet of Yahweh tells Ahab to send an army led by 232 na'arim to face Ben-Hadad, king of Syria, in 1 Kings/3 Kingdoms 20:13–21. This is not presented in the text as a children's crusade. Abraham's 318 elite men, with whom he rescues Lot, are identified as na'arim (Gen. 14:24).

Dozens of other examples from the Hebrew Scriptures could be introduced in support of this definition. Most telling, however, are several usages of the term elsewhere in the Elisha story both before and after this text. When Elisha encounters Naaman, the chief handmaiden of Naaman's wife is identified as a *na'arah*, the feminine form of the noun. Elisha's chief disciple and servant Gehazi is also identified as a na'ar, as are two other unidentified disciples of Elisha, none of whom are portrayed as children (2 Kin./4Kg 5:1–27). Elisha will later send a na'ar to anoint Jehu as king (2 Kin./4Kg 9:1–13).

A further factor has played into the misinterpretation of the identity of this group. The adjective *qatan* is applied to these individuals. The base meaning of this adjective is "little" or "small," and it is then understood to indicate "little children." An examination of the usage of this adjective, however, reveals that it very often does not

---

1   This discussion of the use of *na'ar* owes much to the work of Rodney Cloud.

indicate a small size. In its most prominent usages, it indicates either youth or insignificance. This would mean that we are speaking of young na'arim or low-ranking na'arim. Based on usage throughout the Hebrew Scriptures, the picture is of Elisha on the road encountering a reasonably large group of young Israelite officials, possibly low-ranking military officers.

This group encounters Elisha on the road as they are leaving the city of Bethel. Bethel was the site of one of the two primary high places established by Jeroboam the son of Nebat as a shrine for the worship of golden calves, the other being at Dan (1 Kin./3Kg 12:26–30). The life of Elijah—Elisha's mentor, who had only recently been assumed into the heavenly council of God, passing his prophetic mantle to Elisha—had been consumed with a conflict with the state religion as promulgated by Ahab. Ahab's wife, Jezebel, had brought with her Phoenician religion centered around the worship of Baal and syncretized it with the already idolatrous worship of a version of Yahweh through the calves.

In this setting, the taunts of this group of young toughs as they came upon the prophet walking alone can be seen within this ongoing religious conflict. "Go on up" is a directive to go not only to the city, but to the high place to make a sacrifice. Refusal to participate in the Israelite civil cult had led to the murder of hundreds of prophets of Yahweh at the hands of Ahab's forces (1 Kin./3Kg 18:4). Noncompliance with the demands of this mob to engage in pagan worship would have resulted in Elisha's death, as it had for so many other prophets. The addition of the insult "baldhead" only accentuates the threatening nature of their approach, as it identifies their target as someone unclean and unfit for society.[2]

---

2   Though the relevant terms for baldness are not used frequently enough in the Hebrew Scriptures to be clearly defined as technical terms, the particular term used here, qarat, is worthy of note. This term seems to refer not to baldness of the top of the head, now known as male-pattern baldness, but baldness

When the she-bears emerge, then, it is not to slaughter children for their impropriety, nor is it to avenge Elisha's honor. Rather, these bears emerge to protect Elisha and to save his life from the ancient Israelite equivalent of a violent street gang. While no total number is given for these young officials, that the bears maul forty-two out of their number means that it was more than this. Yahweh protects one faithful prophet when he is confronted and surrounded by a hostile pagan gang intent on forcing him to offer sacrifice to their gods or lose his life.

Within its overarching context, this brief story seems intended to show that just as Yahweh was with Elijah and protected him, so also He now protects Elisha. Though those faithful to the God of Israel are fewer in number and those who serve the powers of darkness hold the power of the state and its military, the creation itself will rise up to defend the righteous. After his rescue, it is not a coincidence that he passes by Carmel, the place of Elijah's great victory against Baal and his prophets, before traveling on to Samaria, capital of the apostate Northern Kingdom, for the battle to continue.

Lot and His Daughters

THE DESTRUCTION OF SODOM AND Gomorrah is challenging from many contemporary perspectives. However troubling it may seem, however, the Scriptures are unequivocal—whenever this event is referred to, it is understood as a manifestation of God's judgment, which extends into the present age and which was demonstrated by the destruction of these cities. Likely the most troubling element of the story has to do with "righteous" Lot's attempts to protect his two angelic visitors from the city's mob. To do this, he appeases the

---

of the back of the head. Its other significant use, Leviticus 13:40, where it is associated with the results of a skin disease, accentuates its use as an insult.

agitators by offering them his unmarried daughters, knowing full well that this will result in their rape and likely murder (Gen. 19:7–8). How could a father do this to his daughters, and how could such a man be considered righteous?

To better understand Lot's actions in their context, the nature of the sin of Sodom must be discussed, which has become hyper-focused on debates regarding homosexual activity. This discussion is not directly germane to understanding Lot's actions.[3] Nevertheless, the way the Scriptures speak of the nexus of oppression, violence, sexual immorality, and the issue of hospitality in Sodom and Gomorrah does directly set the background for the choice that Lot makes in this particular moment. The wickedness of Sodom, which reaches its denouement and a crisis point in this episode, is that to which Lot responds by making this offer of his daughters to the mob.

Rather than enumerating the particular sin(s) of Sodom, the narration leading up to its destruction simply conveys its severity. Their sin is said to be very grave, and Yahweh directly attributes His action to the loud outcry against the city from the victims of its evil (Gen. 18:20). Though Abraham interceded for the city, despite knowing their wickedness (14:22–23), there was not even a handful of righteous in the city, which would have prevented its destruction. To reemphasize this, it is not just a wicked mob that confronts Lot at the door to his home, but every single man in the city (19:4). There is no reason to narrow Sodom's sinfulness to one or even one group of sins. By the time the angels arrived, they were there to rescue Lot and his family, as the city was already going to be destroyed. The narrative takes the time, however, to illustrate the sinfulness of the city. The men of the city gather outside Lot's home with the intent

---

3   Suffice it to say that the condemnation of the sin of the men of Sodom in this
     episode, and elsewhere in the Scriptures where this sin is reflected upon, is
     consistent with the condemnations of homosexual activity in Leviticus 18:22
     and elsewhere.

to capture the two strangers and perpetrate brutal acts of sexual violence against them (19:5, 9).

The majority of subsequent references to Sodom and Gomorrah in the Scriptures refer not to their sins, but to their destruction (Deut. 29:23; Is. 1:9–10; 13:19; Jer. 49:18; 50:40; Lam. 4:6; Amos 4:11; Zeph. 2:9; Matt. 11:23–24; Luke 17:29; 2 Pet. 2:6). Their annihilation is taken as a sort of ultimate threat toward a city consumed by wickedness, that it will be forever laid waste as the cities of the plain were. In other cases, Sodom is held up as a symbol of such a wicked city in comparison to some other city being called to repent or threatened with destruction (Deut. 32:32; Is. 3:9; Rev. 11:8).

A subset of the texts in this latter category makes some statement as to the nature of Sodom's particular sins. The most detailed of these is Ezekiel 16:46–51:

> But your elder sister is Samaria, who dwells with her daughters to the north of you, and your younger sister is Sodom and her daughters to the south of you. But you did not walk in their ways nor according to their abominations, as they were too small, so you became more corrupt than them in every way. As surely as I live, Yahweh says, neither your sister Sodom nor her daughters have done as you and your daughters. See, this was the sin of your sister Sodom: pride, fullness with food, and an abundance of idleness. She and her daughter had these, but the hand of the poor and the needy she in no way strengthened. They were arrogant and committed abominations in my presence. So, I took them away as I saw fit. Samaria did not commit half of your sins, but you have multiplied more abominations than they. Plus, you have justified yourself in all the abominations which you have done.

The focus of this condemnation is twofold. First, the sin of pride and arrogance. Second, the sin of enriching and pleasing oneself at the expense of the poor and needy. Sodom is here said to have been an oppressive civilization that exploited the weak and the powerless and, in her arrogance, justified her actions and refused to repent.

Contemporary debates around sexuality have come to use this passage from Ezekiel to deny that Sodom's sin was sexual in nature— perhaps it was pride or some other sin. This presupposes that exploitation and pride are somehow separate from sexual immorality, with the latter being less serious. A broader picture emerges, however, when other texts that refer to the sins of Sodom are brought into comparison. For example, Jeremiah 23 compares the sins of Jerusalem to those of Sodom. Sodom's sins are here described as "they commit adultery, they walk in lies, and they strengthen the hands of evildoers" (v. 14). This description parallels sexual immorality, treachery, and oppression. The last of these is even described in similar language to that of Ezekiel. When St. Jude refers to the sins of Sodom and Gomorrah, he refers solely to sexual immorality and the "pursuit of strange flesh" (v. 7).

These descriptions of the sins of Sodom are not contradictory. Sins are rarely mutually exclusive—there is no need to single out a specific sin and deem it to be the "real" reason for the destruction of the cities. The use of the particular term "abominations" in Ezekiel at least obliquely references forms of sexual immorality described as abominations in the Torah (as in Leviticus 18). While homosexual activity features in this category, it is by no means the only abomination— sexual exploitation was perhaps a deeper and more pervasive concern in the ancient world. Sexual violence directed by powerful men against women, children, slaves, and other men was used as a means of dominance and oppression. A careful reading of Leviticus 18 reveals that all the commandments of sexual morality are directed toward men to protect women, children, slaves, less powerful men, and others from being used sexually by men who were their superiors in physical strength or societal power. The idea that Sodom's sins and crimes included only violence of a nonsexual nature, or that its victims included only adult women, is dubious at best.

The comments Christ makes about Sodom are useful in drawing these themes together. When Christ sent out both the Twelve (Matt. 11:24) and the Seventy (Luke 10:12), He dispatched them without provisions, expecting they would receive hospitality once they arrived. If they did not, they were to symbolically curse the city with the warning that it will be better for Sodom on the day of judgment than that city.

The hospitality Christ expects his disciples to be shown echoes that which Lot extended to the two angels upon their arrival in Sodom. He meets them at the city gate to welcome them into his home and to give them a place to spend the evening in safety as well as food for their journey (Gen. 19:1–3). As travelers and sojourners, which the men of the city also call Lot (v. 9), they are part of the category of the vulnerable, along with orphans and widows, with whom the God of Israel identifies. There was, in the ancient world, no means of recourse or redress for travelers who might be victimized in a particular city other than God Himself. Hospitality is not a social pleasantry. It is to strengthen the hands of the weak and vulnerable. It is to protect and to provide for them. It is the opposite of victimization and exploitation.

Lot's offer of his daughters takes place within the context of this extension of hospitality. He has placed the two angels, whom he believes to be vulnerable men, under his protection and benefaction (v. 8). His righteous act is not the offering of his daughters for sexual violation, but his protection of the vulnerable and weak, which stands in absolute contrast to the wickedness of the men of Sodom. Righteousness in this case, as in many others already discussed, is a comparative phenomenon. Through the lens of distributive justice, if merely comparing Lot on one side and the men of Sodom on the other, Lot is the righteous party in this instance because he protects rather than seeks to harm the vulnerable. He is not commended as righteous in the sense of being wholly innocent, sinless, or perfect. Indeed, his very presence at the city gates of Sodom, the place where commerce and civil justice take place, indicates that he had become deeply involved with and tainted by the evil of the city. However, he went on to differentiate himself from the rest of the men of the town by his willingness to sacrifice what was precious and valuable to him in order to protect two strangers. It is this differentiation that results in his rescue as the city perishes (vv. 12–13).

To put a finer point on it, it is not the offering of his daughters that is counted as righteous, but rather his preceding actions, namely the safety and sustenance he offered with the motive of protecting strangers. Throughout Lot's life, he suffered the consequences of his choices and actions. His move to dwell near Sodom had resulted in his capture and near enslavement, had Abraham not intervened. His relationship toward his daughters would likewise result in further immorality and chaos. Before this offer in the context of hospitality, Lot had offered his daughters to the men of Sodom in another way. He had betrothed them to men of the city (v. 14). The text of Genesis is placing this in stark contrast to Abraham's desire to find a wife from his own people, not a Canaanite, for Isaac (24:2–4). Lot's failure as a father plays out in his daughters' acts of incest, which would ultimately produce the Moabite and Ammonite peoples, both of whom would become pagan Canaanite foes of Israel.

Jephthah's Daughter

THE BOOK OF JUDGES IS often seen to be problematic as a whole. Certainly, many elements of it need to be deeply couched in euphemism or omitted entirely if its narratives are going to be discussed in an all-ages environment. While large death tolls are described throughout, the descriptions of this violence become increasingly graphic as the book progresses. By the final chapters, the book has descended headlong into the madness of rape, dismemberment, murder, and civil war. Most works of fiction in various media that contain these same elements would be subject to criticism from the perspective of Christian morality. Yet, Judges is a part of the holy Scriptures.

Understanding the Book of Judges as a whole, however, requires understanding its overarching theme and movement. The text begins with failure. The first chapter describes the failure of the tribes of Israel to take the lands allotted to them by Yahweh, their God. He it was who fought for them, so this failure is a failure of their faithfulness. That many chose to enslave the Canaanite population rather than drive them out as they had been commanded is a mark of this disobedience (Judg. 1:28, 30, 33). In response, the Angel of the Lord, who had accompanied Israel from Egypt and dwelt with them for more than forty years, declares His judgment against Israel and departs (2:1–4).[4] Despite a sorrowful reaction to this departure, no repentance took place. Israel as a whole fell to worshipping the Baals of the Canaanites (2:11–13).

In response to Israel's wickedness, foreign invaders were sent to oppress the people as a means of discipline, to attempt to bring about repentance. When the people returned and cried out to their God, He answered by raising up a judge to restore justice by repelling these invaders. Nevertheless, this chastening did not bring about real repentance. The opening of the book lays out the pattern that would repeat itself throughout:

> Yahweh raised up judges who saved them out of the hand of those who pillaged them, but they did not listen to their judges. Instead, they whored after other gods and worshipped them. They quickly

---

4   It is worth noting that here the Angel of Yahweh speaks of both the promises to Abraham and the Exodus in the first person, identifying Himself as Yahweh.

turned from the path in which their fathers had walked, those who had obeyed Yahweh's commandments, and they did not obey them. Whenever Yahweh raised up judges for them, Yahweh was with the judge, and He saved them from the hand of their enemies all the days of the judge. For Yahweh was made compassionate by their groaning, caused by those who punished and oppressed them. But when the judge died, they turned back and were even more wicked than their fathers. They chased other gods by serving them and worshipping them. (Judg. 2:16–19)

Not only did the cycle repeat, but the spiritual condition of the people declined continuously, giving the entire text the pattern of a downward spiral into violence and madness.

The deterioration of Israel's tribes is accompanied by a similar downward trend in the caliber of the men God had called to serve as judges and restore order. Each judge, as the narrative continues, was successively more violent, flawed, and vainglorious. This culminated with Samson, who systematically and unrepentantly violates every element of his Nazirite vows. By the end of the book there is no judge, because Israel's tribes have gone to war with each other rather than a foreign oppressor, bent on taking vengeance and conquering each other. As 1 Samuel/1 Kingdoms begins, the problem is not the final judge, the prophet Samuel, but rather the king, Saul, whom Samuel was pressured into anointing by the people. Israel's death spiral is only finally stopped by David coming to reign as king, and even this respite is brief before another begins that then ends with the destruction of the Northern Kingdom of Israel and the exile of Judah.

Because Judges clearly portrays this downward slide, it is evident that the characters and events in its pages are not intended to serve as positive examples. Increasingly, as the narrative unfolds, the hearer is intended to understand that things are becoming worse and worse. The latter judges and the Israelite civil war of the final chapters of the book are intended to be seen as horrible, a cautionary tale of what happen when Yahweh's commandments are rejected. Judges documents a dark and terrible chapter in Israel's history.

Within this narrative, an episode in the life of Jephthah—a judge from Gilead—is often singled out as particularly troubling. This story, which tells of his clan's deliverance from the Ammonites, is troubling because it involves a human sacrifice. Adding to the complexity, the sacrifice seems to be directed toward Yahweh, the God of Israel. In response to this, many recent commentators have attempted to somehow read the end of the story such that Jephthah does not actually kill and burn his daughter. That he did so, however, is quite clear from the text, and the teaching of the text must be understood, not dodged.

Jephthah is a problematic figure as soon as he is introduced. He is the illegitimate son of the head of his clan, born of a prostitute (Judg. 11:1). The sons of his father's wife, because they were younger, drove Jephthah away to maintain control of the clan against a potential usurper. Jephthah gathered around himself a cadre of mercenaries and criminals (v. 3). The land the Gilead clan dwelled in had belonged to the Ammonites. When the king of Ammon attempted to reclaim it, the elders of Gilead offered to make Jephthah their leader if he would take them into battle against the Ammonites. This is already a break from pattern, because the other judges had been chosen by God for their role. Though God would accomplish His will through Jephthah, Jephthah was chosen not by Him but by the other members of his clan.

In an exchange of messengers that ensues, Jephthah's statements reflect a distorted view of Yahweh, the God of Israel, as merely one God among many national gods. First, he invokes God as a divine witness of a vow made by the elders of Gilead to give Jephthah rule if he is victorious in battle (Judg. 11:10–11). This in itself would be unremarkable and common practice in the ancient world. When the messengers present their cases for ownership of the land, the king of Ammon states the case that this piece of land had formerly belonged to him, and the Israelites had seized it. Jephthah's response is that the God of Israel, Yahweh, had given them the land (v. 23). He continues, however, to state that this is directly parallel to the way Chemosh, the moon god of the Ammonites, had given their land to them (v. 24).

In attributing the possession of the lands of Ammon to Chemosh, Jephthah is directly contradicting Deuteronomy, which states that Yahweh drove out the Rephaim, specifically the giant clan of Zamzummim, before the Ammonites, the sons of Lot, and gave them the land (Deut. 2:19–21). But beyond giving the glory of Yahweh to another, a grievous enough sin in and of itself, Jephthah thereby reduces Yahweh to one territorial god among many, rather than the God who created and rules the heavens and the earth. The author of Judges is here revealing that the religious teaching of the Torah, by the time of Jephthah, was unknown among the people.

After laying out this case, Jephthah announces that Yahweh will be the judge between them as to who is in the right (v. 27). He is here challenging the king of Ammon to what amounts to a collective trial by combat. In the ancient world, it was understood that a battle between peoples was also a contest between their respective gods. While it might be possible to understand this last statement by Jephthah as an affirmation that it was Yahweh alone who would judge and bring about the result, Jephthah's vow is a sign that this is not his understanding. Jephthah offers the Judge of all the earth a bribe.

In the divine battles that accompanied the wars of nations in the ancient world, it was truly rare for any nation, even when suffering a defeat, to perceive their gods as having been overcome by superior force. The far more common interpretation of defeat was that the god or gods had, for some reason or another, abandoned the people, which could even take the form of a god having switched sides during the battle. For this reason, sacrifices and vows were made before entering combat to ingratiate oneself to the gods, who would bring victory or defeat through their sometimes fickle allegiance.

In addressing himself to Yahweh before entering battle, Jephthah does not appeal to the promises made to Abraham. He does not appeal to his own faithfulness to the God of Israel and His commandments. He does not appeal to Yahweh's own glory and His Name and reputation over against His enemies. Instead, he promises a potentially valuable sacrifice. In fact, though often not reflected in English translation, he promises a human sacrifice. He literally says, "If you give the Ammonites into my hand, then whoever comes out of the door of my house to greet me . . . , I will offer him up for a burnt offering" (v. 31). The idea that he believed that a cow or a sheep would come running out to meet him before a human strains credulity and is not how he words the oath.

Jephthah, therefore, intended to sacrifice a human to Yahweh in order to guarantee victory in battle; he just did not intend that human to be his only child, his daughter. Rather than having faith in the righteousness of God, Jephthah was invoking what was seen in the pagan world to be a powerful ritual. In a similar battle situation against Israel, the king of Moab had sacrificed his own son to Chemosh, the same god worshipped by the Ammonites (2 Kin./4Kg 3:27). Far from a sign of piety, Jephthah's oath was an act of sacrilege, and his carrying out the sacrifice of his daughter was an abomination (Judg. 11:39). Her death was not commemorated by the people as a moment of great victory in battle but as a horrific tragedy with four days of mourning every year (v. 40). It is worth noting that this creation of a new feast, not a part of the sacred calendar laid out in the Torah, is itself a sign of the religious ignorance that affected the people.[5]

---

5   Walter Burkert here sees themes that play out in festivals throughout the ancient world revolving around the theme of a "lost virgin." The story of Persephone is another example of these themes. This would imply that the Israelites here, in fact, adopt their own variation of a pagan festival practiced by neighboring nations.

To reinforce this estimation of Jephthah, a second episode in his six-year career as judge is narrated. He led the forces of his clan, Gilead, against the tribe of Ephraim, his fellow Israelites. Identifying them by their accents, Jephthah slaughtered forty-two thousand refugees fleeing the territory he conquered (Judg. 12:5–6). These events both show Jephthah's brutality and anticipate the bloody civil war that would conclude the Book of Judges. He is presented not as a heroic figure but as a violent apostate.

Throughout the story of Jephthah, Yahweh is silent. He takes only one action, as the Spirit empowers Jephthah to be victorious over the Ammonites. This takes place not because of Jephthah's promised sacrifice nor because of any virtue of his but because the God of Israel had indeed given them that land, and He had designated that time to deliver them. He is nowhere said to have acknowledged the act of human sacrifice, let alone accepted it. Judges describes what Jephthah did and ascribes his military victory over the Ammonites, but not over the Ephraimites, to Yahweh. The only evaluation of Jephthah given through the text is a negative one.

Though this understanding is perfectly clear from the text of Judges, critics sometimes object that Jephthah's name is mentioned in Hebrews 11, the famous passage describing heroes of the faith (v. 32). The reference here, however, is ambiguous. Jephthah is not actually praised here for anything. In fact, Hebrews merely states that were it not for time, there would be something to say about Jephthah and several other figures. There is no way of knowing what would have been said. There is no way, even, of knowing to which episode in Jephthah's life reference would have been made.

The list of unmentioned individuals includes other names from Judges, Barak and Samson, who are clearly presented by that text in a negative light. It is easy to imagine, for example, that mention of Barak might well have focused more on praise for Deborah's faith. Likewise, the mention of Jephthah might have focused more on his daughter than on him. His daughter's willingness to go to a sacrificial death is commended occasionally in later tradition, as in Pseudo-Philo. Jephthah himself, however, the Fathers of the Church and Rabbinic Judaism are united in condemning as a rash and ignorant man.

The Sufferings of Job

IT IS NOT A SPECIFIC element or event in the book of Job that is problematic, but rather the overarching premise of the narrative that raises questions, often summarized via caricatures that begin with Job as a good and righteous man leading a quiet and peaceful life. God interrupts this life when He allows Satan to kill his children, destroy his wealth, and even sabotage his physical health. Job ends up on the community's dung heap, scratching at the boils on his body with broken pieces of pottery. Not only does God passively allow this to occur; He does so as what is often characterized as a wager or challenge with Satan to see whether Job will continue to faithfully serve God. This rough, inaccurate description of the action of Job makes it appear that the purpose of the Book of Job is to teach that God causes, or at least allows, human suffering.

Rather, the theme of the Book of Job is God's proclivity to test people. The book enters into the reality of suffering in the world at a personal level. The lion's share of the text consists of interactions between Job, his wife, and his friends as interlocutors. The purpose of the text is to deal with the reality of suffering, a reality that no human can deny. If one acknowledges the existence of the God of Israel, then it is a necessary conclusion that He is at least allowing this suffering to take place, if not bringing it about to some purpose. Job is therefore not making any new claims as to the fact that suffering takes place or to the fact that God allows it. What the text of Job wrestles with is why God allows it and for what purpose He does so.

Job is traditionally classified with the Wisdom Literature of the Old Testament. A primary aim of this literature is to reconcile two seemingly contradictory themes within the Scriptures. These two themes are expressed in the early psalms. Psalm 1 describes the respective fates of the righteous man and the wicked man. The righteous man prospers in all that he does (v. 3). The wicked man, on the other hand, is blown away like chaff (v. 4). In the end, Yahweh knows the way of the righteous, but the way of the wicked dies (vv. 5–6). One might conclude from this element of wisdom that whether one experiences blessings or curses in this life is directly related to personal righteousness or sin. This could further lead to the impression that all those who prosper must be possessors of virtue, while those who suffer are doing so because of their sins.

Psalm 3, from its very beginning, represents a sharp contrast. Though the speaker has put his faith and confidence in Yahweh (vv. 3–4, 8), he is beset by his foes. He is surrounded by many, even thousands, who seek his destruction and who say that God will not save him (vv. 1–2, 6). This leads the speaker to call upon Yahweh to act on his behalf and deliver him from his enemies (v. 7). While it is true that blessing lies in the keeping of God's commandments and destruction and ruin in disobedience, it is also true that in this life in this age, it is often the righteous who suffer and the wicked who prosper. Job is an extended meditation on this contradiction. While Job insists that he is a righteous man suffering in this life unjustly, his interlocutors insist that he must have committed some sin to bring about his calamity.

The answer given by the Book of Job is disclosed by the characterization of its action from the very beginning. The text presents the motivation for God allowing for the activity of Satan in the world to inflict suffering to test His people. "Testing" in this context is not used the way it is commonly understood, however. God does not test

His people in the sense of giving them a pop quiz. He is not conducting an assessment of them in order to gather some information from or about them that He does not already know. God already knows the depths of Job's heart. He created it.

Rather, the way in which this trial or testing takes place is more akin to the "trying" or "testing" of metals that are being smelted and purified. This metaphor is used often in the Scriptures as a description of judgment and trial (e.g., Ps. 66/65:10–12; Is. 48:9–11; Jer. 6:27–30; 9:7–9; Zech. 13:8–9; Mal. 3:2–4; Dan. 11:35; 12:10; 1 Pet. 1:7; Rev. 3:18). Through the trials and adversities of this life, the righteous are refined like precious metals. There is within every human person gold and silver and mud and dross. Life in this age has been given to us for repentance and the pursuit of holiness. As a person draws near to God, the fire of His holiness purges away all that is sinful, wicked, and unclean to reveal, purify, and bring to full beauty what is precious that lies within.

The process of growth in repentance and holiness is painful and difficult, as is coming to physical maturity. It is necessary, however, if one is to come to maturity. This is the answer that the Book of Job ultimately gives in the face of human suffering. Job does not jump through hoops and perform well in God's tests and thereby get his children and wealth replaced. Rather, Job endures great hardship, including the misunderstanding and even mockery of those closest to him. Having come through that hardship and at its depth seen the vision of God Himself, he emerges a holier and wiser man. He has come to know Yahweh more deeply. He has a deeper understanding of the created order. He is able to pass on this wisdom to others who suffer, both as a man and as the protagonist of the book that bears his name. Job at the conclusion of the narrative is greater than when he began. His new wealth and children are emblematic of that growth and change.

Death by Holiness

THE SCRIPTURES CONTAIN SEVERAL INSTANCES in which individuals experience negative consequences—chiefly death—after encountering the sacred. By entering sacred space or coming into contact with holy things improperly, these persons are immediately struck dead. This instantaneous nature of these events leaves no time for repentance or correction. As a result, such deaths—and the warnings issued regarding them, both before and after—have created a certain false sense of fear among many Christians. The seeming injustice of the death penalty for what seems to be minor transgressions has likewise become a source of mockery for critics of the Scriptures and of Christianity.

Before looking at several individual instances of this type from the Scriptures, there is an important overarching distinction to be made. Despite a common interpretive intuition, none of these episodes represents a judgment upon the quality of a particular person. They are not brought about because a person is unworthy, or a sinner, or part of some other category of "wicked humans." There are far more examples in the Scriptures of sinful and unworthy individuals coming into direct contact with God and being brought to repentance or otherwise purified. In fact, this latter description applies to every other contact with God in the Scriptures beyond those represented by the handful about to be discussed.

Rather than the persons involved in these episodes being particularly unworthy or sinful, resulting in their fates, it is that they come into contact with the sacred or come into the presence of God unworthily. It is a question of an adverb rather than an adjective. It is the way in which these persons do what they do that brings upon them the consequences that they receive. The core purpose of religious practice, from the Torah to contemporary Orthodox Christianity, is to describe the means through which, in prayer and repentance, human persons can approach the Holy God and come into contact with the sacred in a way that is purifying and salvific rather than dangerous and therefore fearsome.

Possibly the first notable instance of someone struck dead by the presence of God comes in Leviticus 10. In the preceding chapters, Aaron and his sons had been ordained as priests to serve in that capacity for the nascent nation of Israel. Following their ordination, Aaron had offered sacrifices according to the instructions given him from Yahweh through Moses, and those offerings had been accepted. In the tenth chapter of Leviticus, however, something different occurs in the case of the first offerings of incense made by Aaron's sons Nadab and Abihu.

Nadab and Abihu came to the tabernacle and offered unauthorized incense before Yahweh that He had not commanded (Lev. 10:1). Fire came out from the presence of Yahweh and consumed them, killing them (v. 2). Based only on these first two verses, it is not entirely unclear as to what their specific sin was. There are two obvious possibilities. First, that they were offering the wrong kind of incense, in relation to the specific instructions of Exodus 30. Alternatively, they may have offered this incense at an incorrect time, based on the same instructions. It is also, of course, possible that they did both.

However, Moses gives further information immediately after the deaths by speaking for Yahweh to Aaron and his surviving sons, Eleazar and Ithamar. This information includes a series of specific instructions with warnings that departing from these instructions will result in their deaths. The three specific instructions given to those serving as priests were that they could not have unkempt hair or clothing, they could not come and go from the tabernacle as they wished during their service, and they could not, when coming into the tabernacle, be drunk on wine or strong drink. Finally, they are instructed generally to distinguish between what is sacred and what is profane, what is clean and what is unclean, and to know all the commandments of Yahweh so that they could teach them to Israel (Lev. 10:6–11).

From these descriptions and instructions, the sin of Nadab and Abihu becomes clear. They failed to distinguish between the place they were entering—where dwelt the presence of Yahweh, the God of Israel—from any other tent in the camp. Because they did so, they entered in a casual and impious way. Based on the hints here, they may have been disheveled, drunk, and otherwise careless. This may have extended to the kind of incense they offered or the manner in which they did so. Further, Yahweh through Moses describes their deaths in passive terms—fire comes out and consumes them. The warning is not that God will kill them, but that they will die. The holiness of God is itself dangerous and, therefore, must be approached with care and concern, in the fear of God with faith and love.

Another Old Testament episode brought up in this context is that of Uzzah (2 Sam./2Kg 6:5–11). At the time when David, the prophet and king, brought the ark of the covenant to Jerusalem in preparation for the building of the temple, Uzzah was one of the drivers of the cart that carried it. Famously, as the cart rolled toward Jerusalem, one of the oxen stumbled, jarring the cart. Uzzah reached out and steadied the ark on the cart and was instantly struck dead for his sin. David took this as a sign of Yahweh's disfavor at his actions and ordered the cart to stop and for the ark to remain where it was, on the lands of one Obed-edom the Gittite.[6] God proceeded to bless Obed-edom because of the ark's presence, leading David to finally bring it to Jerusalem, reassured that it was not the moving of the ark that had led to Uzzah's fate.

---

6   As part of Christian theology's identification of the Theotokos as a new ark of the covenant, David's expression of dismay here, "Who am I that the ark of my Lord should come to me?" is echoed in St. Luke's Gospel by St. Elizabeth's exclamation (Luke 1:43). The story regarding the priest Jephonias at the dormition of the Theotokos can therefore be seen to be parallel to that of Uzzah.

The text, therefore, clarifies that the sin was not the transference of the ark, but rather Uzzah's touching it in order to steady it. As already seen in the case of Nadab and Abihu, the issue here is Uzzah treating the ark as any other object he might haul in his cart. Of course, the ark is not just another box or a valuable golden piece of art, but the locus of Yahweh's presence among the people of Israel.

At a previous point in the ark's history, the ark had been returned by the Philistines to the Israelites on an unmanned cart (1 Sam./1Kg 6:7–12). When we compare these two episodes, the contrast is obvious. The pagan Philistines had a greater degree of belief and trust in Yahweh than Uzzah. It was not, therefore, some unworthiness or sinfulness of Uzzah in particular that brought about his demise. Rather, it was his casual treatment of the ark of God's holiness and how he interacted with it.

In the New Testament, an episode in the Acts of the Apostles closely parallels that of Nadab and Abihu, and deliberately so. Ananias and Sapphira, two members of the church at Jerusalem at its earliest phase, sold a tract of land. They brought a portion of the proceeds to the apostles and gave it to the Christian community. When St. Peter asked if the donation represented the entire sum of the sale, both Ananias and his wife separately lied and were each struck dead. In both cases, St. Peter states before their demise that they have lied to God, the Holy Spirit (Acts 5:1–11). The text is clear that it was the falsehood that was the sin, not the percentage of the money that they chose to donate.

In the same way in which the story of Nadab and Abihu follows the consecration of the tabernacle, in which it was filled by the presence of Yahweh, the story of Ananias and Sapphira follows the outpouring of the Spirit on Pentecost upon the members of the community in Jerusalem. Nadab and Abihu's deaths served as a warning to the community as a whole, and the priests in particular, that they must carefully discern the way they approached the presence of

God. Similarly, the deaths of Ananias and Sapphira remind the entire Christian community that the presence of the Spirit in the Church requires the same level of devotion and care required of the priests of the Old Covenant when an approach is made to the God of Israel.

Saint Paul applies this theology in his instructions regarding the Eucharist (1 Cor. 11:27–32). He speaks of the manner in which one approaches the Eucharist. To receive unworthily is to eat and drink judgment. As before, this is not a prohibition of certain people whom St. Paul deems "unworthy" to partake of the Eucharist. Rather, it is a reminder of the dangerous nature of drawing close to God. It is a reaffirmation by St. Paul that to eat and drink of the Eucharist is to receive the Body and Blood of Christ, of God Himself, within one's own body. There is no more intimate contact with the Triune God. Doing this in a casual or otherwise unworthy way, without repentance, had led to some in the community at Corinth becoming ill, and even to the point of death.

Did a Rape Victim Have to Marry Her Rapist?

IT HAS BECOME A STANDARD line of attack much repeated by atheistic opponents of Christianity and opponents of the Old Testament in general that somewhere in its pages, the Old Testament requires rape victims to marry their perpetrators. It is not entirely clear how this view of Scripture originated or what passage it refers to, but the most likely possibility is Deuteronomy 22:22–28. While this passage occurs within other commandments concerning sexual immorality, it is less concerned with moral definitions of sexual immorality and more so with how to deal with this evil in the context of the community after it has occurred.

The way that the Torah speaks of women is itself the cause of discomfort to many modern readers. Women are talked about in the same way that children are, almost as objects or possessions. Critics tend to interpret this as the Scriptures, and by extension the Christian God, denying women's agency. The reality on the ground in the late Bronze Age, however, is that women had been robbed of their agency by every culture then existing, including that of ancient Israel. Even though they were completely robbed of control and decision-making power in their own lives, women in the ancient world were then also objects of blame, particularly in regard to sexual transgressions. Through the commandments of the Torah, Yahweh, the God of Israel, protected women from this blame.[7] All the Torah's commandments regarding sexual immorality are directed to men because they held the power in the social interactions. Cultures formed by Christianity have come to acknowledge and respect women's agency, and this is welcome. This equal standing brings with it an equal responsibility to the commandments of God.

Deuteronomy 22:22–28 begins by reiterating the commandment against adultery as a basic component of what constitutes sexual immorality. If a man is found to be engaging in sexual relations with another man's wife, both are to be put to death to purge this evil from Israel (Deut. 22:22). This scenario is followed by two different cases in which a man and woman may be caught engaged in an adulterous act. The first involves a man engaging in sexual activity with a woman who is betrothed—not married—to another man in the city; this is treated as adultery and incurs the usual penalty. If, however, in the second case this same situation is discovered outside of a city, the woman is not punished, but only the man.

---

7   In addition to these commandments of the Torah, descriptions of actual incidents in the Scriptures enact protection of women from blame for male transgressions. In the story of Susanna, the prophet Daniel speaks on behalf of the God of Israel to protect a woman falsely accused (Daniel chapter 1 in the Greek versions). Christ Himself intervenes to prevent the stoning of the woman taken in adultery (traditionally located in John 7:53—8:11). In both of these cases, the idea that the male parties involved bare responsibility is suspiciously absent.

The distinction here between city and countryside hinges on whether the woman was able to cry out for help (Deut. 22:24, 27). It should be noted that the issue is not whether she cried for help, but whether she could have been heard if she had. The woman is not interrogated or questioned in any way. In modern legal proceedings to resolve these crimes, the victim is frequently called to testify publicly and to suffer further public humiliation. The procedure described here in the Torah protects women from this further victimization. If the act occurred in a place where she could not have been heard, she is given the benefit of the doubt and assumed not to be complicit. Because the man involved occupied the position of power in ancient society, he is, in all cases, held to be guilty and subject to the death penalty.

Both examples convey two important principles of the Torah, which represent massive progress in the treatment of women in the ancient Near East. First, a woman who has protected her chastity but is sexually assaulted is completely innocent. Essentially, in the eyes of the Torah, she is still a virgin. This means that her betrothal is still valid, and she was able to, in ancient Israelite culture, be part of a lawful marriage. Her rape is here equated with murder (Deut. 22:26). She bears no more guilt or shame than a murder victim. Second, this gives women the benefit of the doubt. A woman did not have to prove her resistance or rejection of the man's advances. In the case of a rape accusation in which it is her word against his with no other evidence, her word is to be believed, and only the man is to be treated as sexually immoral and executed.

Thus far, it is clear that the Torah takes a different position on rape than the original question presupposes—it does not compel a woman who has been raped to marry her perpetrator. It becomes confusing, however, when conflated with the command that follows in Deuteronomy 22:28–29 regarding the responsibilities of a man to a woman whose virginity he has taken. This command serves a different purpose than the ones that preceded it. While the former sought to advance the innocence of betrothed rape victims and prevent their punishment, the latter is aimed at preventing the sexual exploitation of unmarried young women (vv. 28–29).

That it is unrelated is clear in that the case discussed by this regulation is not punished by death or any other form of penalty. Further, the woman's consent is not at issue because her societal guilt or shame is not at issue. No one accuses the woman discussed in Deuteronomy 22:28–29 of anything. The idea that this case has something to do with sexual assault may be derived from an overinterpretation of the English word "seize," used in several translations. The Hebrew word can simply mean "take" or "acquire."[8] The case, then, is merely one in which a man takes to himself an unbetrothed virgin, engages in sexual conduct with her, and this is discovered (v. 28).

In this instance, the man is required to pay somewhat higher than the typical dowry to her father and marry her. He is not allowed to divorce her under any circumstances. Because the concept of sexual consent, as we understand it in the contemporary world, did not exist within the ancient world, it is entirely possible that a substantial number of these virgin women did not consent to the sexual activity they were found to have engaged in. From the vantage point of understandings of marriage and family in the modern world, to require those women to be married to the man who potentially raped them seems deeply troubling indeed.

Once again, however—and it is worth repeating in this difficult case—the ancient world was not the modern world. In Bronze and Iron Age cultures, women did not pursue careers. The entire modern capitalist system of having a job for an employer did not exist. In

---

8   It is also possible that this interpretation comes from the LXX rendering. One use of the Hebrew word here is "to take a city." The Greek translates this word with a word often used to mean "besiege" or "conquer." Given the present context, the Greek might be best translated as referring to a man who seduces a woman to have sexual relations with her.

these agrarian cultures, extended family units worked the land for their own survival. Tracts of land were passed down from fathers to sons, though the Torah (alone in its era) makes provision for daughters to inherit when there are no sons in order to keep lands in particular clans and tribes (see Num. 36:5–11). A woman's life in these cultures, therefore, began as a part of the family of her father and grandfather then transitioned to being a part of the family of her husband. It is for this reason that widows, like orphans, belonged to the vulnerable segments of Israelite society.

It is this understanding that undergirds the idea of a dowry or "bride price." It is not a question of women being treated as property. Rather, in such an agrarian society, a daughter is seen to be a valuable part of her family in working the land and helping to provide for its needs. When a new husband took a woman from her father's house, he was depriving the father of someone of real value. He was making life more difficult for her family of origin. The dowry, then, was a way of compensating a father for the loss of his daughter. Its payment was more like a settlement in a civil case than a retail transaction.

Also, in these societies, for a contracted marriage to be valid, the woman was required to be a virgin, to have maintained her chastity until her wedding day. Both young women and men in these societies were typically married between the ages of twelve and fourteen. If therefore, a woman had engaged in some form of fornication, she would be unable to contract a legal marriage. This would mean that at the death of her father, she would be left without home or means of support. Women in such a situation would have only two options for survival: begging or prostitution.

Therefore, in ancient Israel, if a man took an unmarried woman's virginity under any circumstances, he had violated justice. He had done lasting damage to the woman, who would now be unable to contract a legal marriage. This was damage that could not be undone. In addition, he had done damage to her whole family and their family life. And the ripple effects of his selfish actions in pursuing the satisfaction of his desires moved out from there into the whole community. To restore justice, then, he was required to pay damages to the woman's family first of all.

More importantly, he was now required to support and provide for her for the rest of her life. It must be remembered that in ancient Israel, each of the twelve tribes consisted of clans, and each clan consisted of a number of extended families. Though we think in terms of nuclear families, a married couple and children, this was rare in the ancient world. Even in families in which polygamy was not being practiced, family units included grandparents, parents, children, aunts, uncles, and cousins. They also included indentured servants who lived on and assisted in working the land. A woman who was married under these circumstances would have joined this extended family and become one of the people for whom the head of that family was responsible. She would have been added to the household whether she, going forward, had any personal relationship with her husband or not. Regardless, he is not allowed to divorce her.

By taking away her possibility at a normal future, a man became responsible for a woman's future. He could not simply use her to satisfy his sexual desires and then leave her, damage done, to fend for herself. The principle at play here in the Torah is comparable to modern child support compensation. If a man impregnates a woman, he is responsible for the care and support of the child until the child becomes a self-supporting adult. In ancient cultures, women were just as vulnerable as children are in modern cultures. Men were allowed to do with unmarried women as they pleased with little to no consequence. The Torah applies justice to this situation, protecting women from use, exploitation, and abandonment.

God and Violence

A T THE CREATION OF THE heavens and the earth, the Triune
God established order and justice in the world with Eden as an
outpost. Humanity was entrusted with bringing the work of creation
to completion through cooperation with Him. Just as in the first three
days of creation God had set the world in order and in another three
had filled it with life, so also humanity was created to fill the earth
and subdue it. Instead, humanity joined in the rebellion of the fallen
spiritual powers. Rather than bringing life and justice to the world,
humans have instead brought further chaos, destruction, injustice,
and death.

In response, God has not abandoned His creation. He has not
destroyed humanity to purify creation for Himself. He did not immediately consign humanity to the lake of fire prepared for the devil
and his angels. Rather, in the Person of Jesus Christ, He entered His
creation in order to justify it, to reconcile it to Himself, and to free
humanity from the destructive consequences of human sin, including death. In doing so, Christ Himself suffered the entirety of evil,
rejection, hatred, and suffering this world has to offer, which culminated in a torturous and humiliating death. It was by His own death
that Christ trampled down death and made powerless the devil.

The world in which we live, the only world that is currently real, is
filled with suffering and pain, with tears and death. It is not this way

because God made it this way, but because we have made it this way. And we continue to do so. The Scriptures are historically located. Where they are not communicating the history of this world, they were written by humans in this world, speaking in and navigating it with all its darkness. It is into our world that Christ came to once again establish justice. He came to purify His creation of the stain of sin and wickedness. He came so that death would die.

A world filled with violence needs correction, and its correction is a violent one. The evils of violence and oppression are not purely accidental. They do not represent blind mistakes or naïve errors on the part of finite human beings. They are not the result of some flaw in our makeup over which we are powerless. Rather, they are deliberate acts of rebellion and hatred against God, who is life and love. They represent the violent acting out of self-exclusion from the light of God's life. Unlike the demonic beings with whom this rebellion began, humanity was granted a reprieve. Life in this world, with all its darkness, represents divine grace and a chance for repentance.

Christ came into this world to save us. He did not come, as some theological positions might suggest, to save us from the Father, or from the violence He or the Father would perpetrate against us if He had not come. He came to save us from our sins. He came to save us not from Himself but from ourselves. He came to save His creation from destruction at our hands. He came to save the victims—past, present, and future—from our own hands, even when the victim is at times our very selves.

> But God shows his love for us in that while we were still sinners, Christ died for us. Because, therefore, we have now been justified by His blood, much more shall we be saved by Him from the wrath of God. For if while we were enemies, we were reconciled to God by the death of His Son, much more, now that we are reconciled, shall we be saved by His life. (Rom. 5:8–10)

Scripture Index

Note: The Old Testament books are ordered according to the Western, Protestant reckoning. For chapters and verses which differ between the Hebrew and Greek versions, the Hebrew is listed first, followed by the Greek after a backslash. Extracanonical books are gathered together at the end. Discussions about specific books as a whole can be found in the subject index.

Old Testament

138

Subject Index

Note: Discussions of biblical and extracanonical books are included in this subject index. References to specific chapters and verses can be found in the Scripture index.

A

Aaron, 22, 100–101, 125

Abel, 44, 45. *See also* Cain

Abihu and Nadab, 53, 125–26, 127

Abraham, 42, 74, 75n3, 98–99, 107, 110, 114

Adam and Eve, 30–32, 40, 44, 45, 49

adultery, 129. *See also* sexual immorality

Ahab, 107, 108

allegory, and biblical interpretation, 9–11, 61, 79–80

Amalekites, 74, 75, 77, 88

Ammonites, 74, 114, 117–18, 120

Amorites (Martu), 71, 75–76

Anakim, 77. *See also* giants

Ananias and Sapphira, 127–28

ancient world: kings and justice, 17–18; sexual violence and exploitation, 112–13; universality of Flood and other stories, 69–70; war, 83, 84–85, 89–90, 94–95, 118–19; women, 129, 131–33

Angel of the Lord, 4, 115, 115n4

apkallu, 70

Aramaic Targums, 46n3, 47

archaeology, 9–10

ark of the covenant, 88, 92, 126–27, 126n6

Assyrians, 2, 92, 94

Atlantis, 69

atonement (blood atonement): Day of Atonement, 43n1, 50–51, 52–53, 53–56, 57, 58–59; debates over, 43, 43n1; Jesus Christ and, 56, 59–60; other uses of blood, 56–58; Passover and, 58–59

Augustine of Hippo, 30, 46n4

Azazel, 55, 59

B

Babylonians, 2, 32, 59, 70, 85

Balaam, 90

baldness, 108n2

Josephus, 45–46, 46n2, 47, 48
Joshua, 4, 18, 64, 80, 91
Joshua, Book of, 9, 61–62, 74, 87, 88
Judas Iscariot, 102n3
judges, 18–19, 25, 115–16
Judges, Book of, 86, 114–17
Julius Caesar, 95
justice and judgment, divine:
    about, 13–15; blessing from, 17;
    corruption from being unjust,
    17, 24; death and, 33–35, 38;
    of devil and demons, 65–66;
    distributive, retributive, and
    social justice, 15–16; evil and,
    24–25; against giants, 74–78,
    88–89, 96, 118; indication of in
    Scriptures, 86–87; Jesus Christ
    and, 14, 19–20; justification and,
    26–27; kings and, 17–19; Last
    Judgment and, 23–24, 25–26;
    as original state of created order,
    19; protection of poor, weak, and
    oppressed, 20–23; terminology,
    13–14; in Torah, 16–17. *See also*
    sin; spiritual warfare; war, holy
justification, 23, 26–27

K
kings, 17–19, 91–92

L
Lamech (Cain's descendant),
    46–47, 46n4, 70
Lamech (Noah's father), 44
Last Judgment, 23–24, 25–26
Law. *See* Torah
Levites, 100, 101

Leviticus, 59
Lotan, 75
Lot and his daughters, 109–10,
    113–14
Luke, Gospel of, 80

M
Maccabees, 102
Manifest Destiny, 62–63, 62n1
Marcion, vi, vin1
Mark, Gospel of, 80
Martu. *See* Amorites
Mary, Mother of God (Theotokos),
    126n6
Matthew, Gospel of, 80
Melchizedek, 99
mercy and compassion, 14, 25–26
Michael (archangel), 65, 68
mishpat (justice), 17, 17n1
Moabites, 74, 114, 119
morality, 2, 85–86. *See also* sexual
    immorality
Moses, 18, 22, 75, 99, 100–102, 125
Mount Sinai, 75

N
na'ar (*na'arim*), 106–7
Nadab and Abihu, 53, 125–26, 127
Nephilim, 70, 75, 81.
New Testament, 4–5, 8, 62, 78–80,
    82. *See also* Jesus Christ; Paul
Nietzsche, Friedrich, 5n2
Noah. *See* Flood
Numbers, 74

O
Og (king of Bashan), 72, 75–76

Author
Biography

FATHER STEPHEN is the author of *The Religion of the Apostles* from Ancient Faith Publishing and is also the pastor of Archangel Gabriel Orthodox Church (Antiochian) in Lafayette, Louisiana. He holds a PhD in Biblical Studies from Amridge University and is the host of *The Whole Counsel of God* podcast and co-host of the *Lord of Spirits* podcast on Ancient Faith Radio. He is also the author of *The Whole Counsel Blog* on the Ancient Faith Ministries website. Father Stephen wrote this book in response to requests for an Orthodox perspective on violence in the Old Testament.

Lord of Spirits Podcast
The Seen and Unseen World in Orthodox Christian Tradition

The modern world does not acknowledge but is nevertheless haunted by spirits—angels, demons, and saints. Orthodox Christian priests Fr. Andrew Stephen Damick and Fr. Stephen De Young host this live call-in show focused on enchantment in creation, the union of the seen and unseen as made by God and experienced by mankind throughout history.

The live edition of this show airs on the second and fourth Thursdays of the month at 7:00 P.M. ET / 4:00 P.M. PT. Tune in at Ancient Faith Radio.

The Whole Counsel of God Podcast
Verse by Verse through the Scriptures

This podcast takes us through the Holy Scriptures in a verse-by-verse study based on the Great Tradition of the Orthodox Church. These studies were recorded live at Archangel Gabriel Orthodox Church in Lafayette, Louisiana, and include questions from his audience.

https://www.ancientfaith.com/podcasts/wholecounsel

The Whole Counsel Blog
The Scriptures in the Orthodox Church

In this blog, Fr. Stephen De Young examines biblical subjects and themes through the lens of the Great Tradition of the Orthodox Church.

https://blogs.ancientfaith.com/wholecounsel/

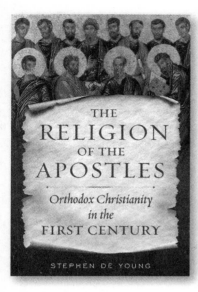

The Religion of the Apostles
Orthodox Christianity in the First Century

Reverend Dr. Stephen De Young traces the lineage of Orthodox Christianity back to the faith and witness of the apostles, which was rooted in a first-century Jewish worldview. *The Religion of the Apostles* presents the Orthodox Christian Church of today as a continuation of the religious life of the apostles, which in turn was a continuation of the life of the people of God since the beginning of creation.

store.ancientfaith.com

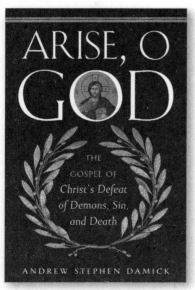

Arise, O God
The Gospel of Christ's Defeat of Demons, Sin, and Death

The gospel of Jesus Christ is not about what Jesus can do for your life. It is not even the answer to the question, "How can I be saved?" It is the declaration of a victory. In His coming to earth, His suffering, and His Resurrection, Christ conquered demons, sin, and death. In *Arise, O God*, author and podcaster Fr. Andrew Stephen Damick introduces us to the spiritual war that Christ won by His victory, how we are caught in that war's cosmic crossfire, what the true content of the gospel is—and how we are to respond.

store.ancientfaith.com

Ancient Faith Publishing hopes you have enjoyed and bene-fited from this book. The proceeds from the sales of our books only partially cover the costs of operating our nonprofit min-istry—which includes both the work of **Ancient Faith Pub-lishing** and the work of **Ancient Faith Radio**. Your financial support makes it possible to continue this ministry both in print and online. Donations are tax-deductible and can be made at **www.ancientfaith.com**.